THE JUNCTION

Tomas Venclova was born in Klaipėda, Lithuania in 1937. He graduated from Vilnius University in 1960. From 1956 on, Venclova took part in the Lithuanian and Soviet dissident movements, making friends with Joseph Brodsky, Natalia Gorbanevskaia, and other participants in the Soviet underground. He made his living by translating Baudelaire, Saint John-Perse, T.S. Eliot, Dylan Thomas, W.H. Auden, Robert Frost, Anna Akhmatova, Osip Mandelstam and many others into Lithuanian. Venclova was one of the five founding members of the Lithuanian Helsinki group, and in 1977 he emigrated.

He has taught Russian and Polish literature, as well as Lithuanian language, at Yale University, since 1985. Considered one of the major figures of world poetry, his work has been translated by Czesław Miłosz into Polish and by Joseph Brodsky into Russian. His published works include volumes of poetry, criticism, literary biography, conversations and works on Vilnius. He has been the recipient of a numerous awards including the Lithuanian National Prize in 2000, the 2002 Prize of Two Nations, which he received jointly with Czesław Miłosz, the 2005 Jotvingiai Prize, and the New Culture of New Europe Prize, 2005.

He holds a number of honorary doctorates, and was chosen for Poland's Borderland Award (2001), which promotes the study and popularisation of an author's work. Venclova's poetry has been translated into more than 20 languages, including Hebrew, Chinese, and Albanian. He is active in the contemporary cultural life of Lithuania, and is one of its most well respected figures.

His books in English include: *Aleksander Wat: Life and Art of an Iconoclast* (Yale University Press, 1996); an earlier selection of poems translated by Diana Senechal, *Winter Dialogue* (Northwestern University Press, 1997); a collection of essays, *Forms of Hope* (Sheep Meadow Press, 1999); and *The Junction: Selected Poems*, edited by Ellen Hinsey, translated by Ellen Hinsey, Constantine Rusanov and Diana Senechal (Bloodaxe Books, 2008).

For notes on the translators, please see page 168.

TOMAS VENCLOVA

THE JUNCTION
SELECTED POEMS

EDITED BY ELLEN HINSEY

TRANSLATED BY ELLEN HINSEY,
CONSTANTINE RUSANOV & DIANA SENECHAL

BLOODAXE BOOKS

Copyright © Tomas Venclova 1997, 2005, 2008
Selection, introduction and notes copyright © Ellen Hinsey 2008
Translations pages 17-77 copyright © Ellen Hinsey & Constantine Rusanov 2008
Translations pages 79-156 © Diana Senechal 1997, 2008

ISBN: 978 1 85224 810 9

First published 2008 by
Bloodaxe Books Ltd,
Highgreen,
Tarset,
Northumberland NE48 1RP.

www.bloodaxebooks.com
For further information about Bloodaxe titles
please visit our website or write to
the above address for a catalogue.

Bloodaxe Books Ltd acknowledges
the financial assistance of
Arts Council England, North East.
Thanks are also due to Arts Council England
for a translation grant for this book.

Cover design: Neil Astley & Pamela Robertson-Pearce.

Printed in Great Britain by
Bell & Bain Limited, Glasgow, Scotland.

ACKNOWLEDGEMENTS

Acknowledgement is made to the following publications in which selections of this work have previously appeared or are forthcoming:

Poetry Review:
  'Dunes at Watermill'
Poetry Review / Contemporary Lithuanian Poets Supplement:
  'The Émigré'
  'Anno Domini 2002'
  'On the Boulevard by Town Hall'
Poetry:
  'In the Lake Region'
The Irish Times:
  'Ormond Quay'
Modern Poetry in Translation:
  'Arrival in Atlantis'
  'Discipline and Punish. A Visit to the Detention Centre IZ-45/1'
  'Homage to Shqiperia'
The New England Review:
  'A New Postcard From the City of K.'
  'Verses for a Child's Birth'
Agni Review
  'For R.K.'
  'The Opposite Shore (Užupis)'
Cúirt Annual (Cúirt International Festival of Literature):
  'The Junction'
Publication of the 37th Poetry International Festival (Rotterdam):
  'After the Lecture'
  'The Junction'
  'From Landwehrkanal to Spree'
  'Antonio Vivaldi'
Ars Interpres:
  'After the Lecture'
  'Landscape 2001'
  'Theseus Leaving Athens'
  'Two Apocrypha'
  'Commentary'
  'Anno Domini 2002'

Lituanus:
  'From Landwehrkanal to Spree'
Metamorphoses:
  'Henkus Hapenčkus, In Memoriam'
  'San Michele'
Partisan Review:
  'The Member of the Landing Crew'
  'A View From an Alley'

'The Junction', 'After the Lecture', 'Song of the Borderland', 'On the Boulevard near Town Hall', 'Two Apocrypha', 'Antonio Vivaldi', 'Theseus Leaving Athens' and 'Landscape, Summer 2001' also appeared in *Wiersze Sejnenskie* (Sejny Poems), a trilingual volume published by the Borderland Foundation, Sejny, Poland.

'San Michele' also appeared in *Baltic Poets*, ed. Juris Kronbergs (Stockholm, Swedish Institute, 1999).

'Member of the Landing Crew' also appeared in *Orient Express*, *Krasnogruda*, *Lituanus* and *Baltic Poets*, ed. Juris Kronbergs (Stockholm: Swedish Institute, 1999).

'A View from an Alley' also appeared in *Krasnogruda*, *Vilnius* and *Lithuania in Her Own Words: An Anthology of Contemporary Lithuanian Writers* (Vilnius: 1997).

Some poems, collected here under 'The Junction' and 'Winter Dialogue' were first published in other selected volumes in Lithuanian. A full list of publication sources appears at the end of this book.

Grateful acknowledgement is made to Northwestern University Press for their permission to reprint poems from *Winter Dialogue*, translated by Diana Senechal (1997). Poems in this collection may appear in revised form.

CONTENTS

TOMAS VENCLOVA
The Labours of Poetry:
Between Classicism and Ruins *by* ELLEN HINSEY

In Herodotus' *Histories* one finds the story of the two Spartans who offer themselves in atonement for a wrong committed by their democratic society. The tyrant who receives them tries to dissuade them from such extreme measures, suggesting instead that they switch sides and accept to live under tyranny. Their response, among the most moving in the history of world literature, is not only poignant but astounding: 'You who have not experienced liberty do not know if it is sweet or not. If you knew what freedom was, you would advise us to fight for it not just with spears but with battle axes.' For the text, written nearly 2,500 years ago, has already established the essential coordinates of an ethical geometry that remain valid to this day: at the base is the conflict between individual conscience and the threat of tyranny. And above both, in the freedom of the telling of the story, floats the word.

Tomas Venclova, one of the last of a generation of poets in the great European tradition, is a writer with a lived experience of both tyranny and the power of the word. Born on 11 September 1937 in Klaipėda, Lithuania, he took his degree (interrupted for a time due to 'forbidden' literary activities) in Lithuania's capital city of Vilnius. He continued his studies in semiotics and Russian literature at the university of Tartu, returning to the University of Vilnius to teach. In addition to writing poetry and literary criticism, he translated writers such as T.S. Eliot, W.H. Auden, Dylan Thomas, Charles Baudelaire and Osip Mandelstam into Lithuanian. During this period he also travelled extensively in the Eastern Bloc, in particular to Moscow and Leningrad, where he made the acquaintance of the great Silver Age Russian poets Anna Akhmatova and Boris Pasternak, as well as a generation of younger poets, including Natalia Gorbanevskaia and Joseph Brodsky, who would become lifelong friends. Already in strong disagreement with Soviet policies following the 1956 invasion of Hungary, his outspoken involvement in the 70s with dissident politics – which included being a founding member of the Lithuanian Helsinki Group – led to a ban on publishing, exile in the West, and the stripping of his Soviet citizenship in 1977.

Joseph Brodsky, in his essay on Venclova's work, 'Poetry as a Form of Resistance to Reality',[1] observed that Venclova's involvement in such dissident activities 'bordered on foolhardiness'. This remark is best understood in light of Lithuania's particular fate in the second half of the 20th century. Venclova was born during the long-fought for but short-lived independence that Lithuania experienced during the interwar period 1918–40. At the start of the Second World War, Tomas and his parents were forced to leave Klaipėda (formerly the German city of Memel, occupied by Germany early in the war) and were relocated to Lithuania's interwar capital, Kaunas. In 1940, the entire country was annexed by the Soviet Union, and during the first year of the war an estimated 17,000 Lithuanians were deported by the Russians. In June 1941, the country was invaded by Germany. During this period the Venclova family members were separated, and Tomas's mother was briefly arrested. Over the next four years, more than 170,000 Lithuanians would be killed, including almost the entire Jewish population of the country. In the summer of 1944 when the Germans retreated, the Soviets reoccupied Lithuania, and while the exact number of those deported to Siberian labour camps at the end of the war and up until Stalin's death is disputed, it is estimated at 140,000,[2] of which approximately 30 percent perished. The vice-like grip of these successive occupations, and the 'long historical winter' that followed in its wake, greatly suppressed Lithuanian culture and national aspirations. At the time of Venclova's participation in the fragile dissident movement in 1976, support of Lithuanian human rights was indeed foolhardy. The country's independence still lay another decade and a half in the future.

Venclova's experience of growing up in the shadow of these post-war ruins is an integral part of his work. For, as in many European cities, the ruin that surrounded him was not merely metaphorical: in his writings he tells how, on his very first day of school, he got lost in Vilnius' ruins and wandered for four hours in search of his house. Half of the city was destroyed, and on certain streets, every other house was burned out. Yet by some miracle, all the city's churches had survived, together with certain other monuments from the capital's architectural past. As a young man, Venclova came to regard these vestiges as a sign – one that 'made a statement and exacted a demand'.[3] During the years of Communist monotony and repression, he memorised Vilnius's architectural details down to the last window frame and column, and at difficult moments in his life he would stand in one of the city's squares and allow the sheer presence of their historical continuity to lift his spirit. These vestiges represented the remains of a coherent world, a world that – however far off that eventuality might be – could one day, given enough patience, rise from the debris.

If it can be said that formal choices for poets are an extension of autobiography and a reflection of intimate belief, a reading of Venclova's work affirms how such a firsthand encounter with destruction can have the counter-effect of forging a driven uprightness. This personal and aesthetic credo was further strengthened by the moral compromises Venclova witnessed close to hand, not the least of which were those made by his father, a high-ranking Soviet official and poet, to whom he addresses a conflicted, poignant elegy in *The Junction*. After leaving Lithuania, Venclova travelled in Europe and in the United States, taking a position at Yale University, where he has been a professor of Slavic Languages and Literatures for the past 25 years. During this period in exile he continued to write poetry, which has been translated into more than 20 languages. He has also written literary biography, cultural commentary and essays, many of which concern the fates of persecuted writers. Throughout his work he addresses the lived experience of totalitarianism and the lessons and warnings that can be gleaned from its dark historical passage.

But, the uprightness one finds in Venclova's work is not only ethical, but also material and concrete – it is the technical basis out of which his poems arise. Long ago Venclova chose as his poetic vehicle a modern and "rebellious" form of classicism. While the formality of his poems might at first glance seem anachronistic to the Western reader, over time the implications of their logic become urgently clear. For Venclova's brand of classicism has nothing to do with political conservatism (as the aesthetic is sometimes portrayed in the West) but rather the contrary: it is a way to preserve the conditions that give rise to freedom of thought, democracy and culture in general. Throughout the course of his *oeuvre* Venclova has affirmed that, in the face of the destructive forces of history, one of poetry's tasks is to be 'filled to the limits with harmony and sense, so that it might resist the monotony and predictability of the world outside'.[4] For Venclova, as well as for other poets with whom he shares this poetic vision, including Anna Akhmatova, a poem's clarity, rhythm, syntax and composition constitute in themselves a moral task.

To this end, Venclova's poems employ a vast range of traditional forms and techniques, including variations on metrical schemes, intricate rhyme strategies and other resources from poetry's inheritance. These technical elements are set against the poems' contents and landscapes. If in his earlier volume of selected poems in English, *Winter Dialogue*, there is a concern with endurance, and a search for absolutes in the face of adverse conditions both in Lithuania and in exile, in his most recent work we find the figure of a poet returning from exile, surveying what has occurred, what buildings still stand, and the fates of those one loved. And while these poems are filled with melancholy at the passage of time and the poignancy of anticipated mortality, there is also a sense of affirmation. For despite everything, each element that is salvaged constitutes a form of victory. And in this light Venclova's poems, with their stanzas that fit one atop the other, begin to appear like classical columns, which slowly rise towards the mythical silence where Venclova believes poetry begins and ends. His poems at once harbouring the memory of culture and becoming an enactment of culture itself – a testimony to all that can be, and is, preserved from the vicissitudes of History.

Understandably, the task that Venclova has set himself is a formidable one. And there are times when it seems that the poet believes that by sheer will and virtuoso technique alone, the tottering ruins of the world can be held together – just. Yet Venclova also allows for the possibility that this spiritual, philosophical and moral challenge might fail. And in the end, despite his cautious optimism, he perceives in this neither cause for surprise nor ultimate despair. A metaphysical poet, his work maintains the traditional task of the writer's reflections on ultimate things that began before us and will exist after us, and thereby makes peace with the uncertain future that we create for ourselves. If classicism is the vehicle for Venclova's craft, then his voice – the wise and patient voice that inhabits this poetic world – is not unlike that of Zeno of Citium, who sat teaching beneath the columns of the *stoa*'s portico in ancient Athens. For Venclova's philosophy is not far from that of the Stoics who espoused the idea that good lies in the soul itself, in wisdom and self-control, and believed in a detachment that embraced pain and misfortune, life and death.

At the end of his most recent book in Lithuanian, *Sankirta* (*The Junction*), there is a poem in which the poet visits the lake district on the outskirts of Berlin, and stands on the shores of the Wannsee, home to the conference house in which the Nazis consolidated policy for the extermination of Europe's Jews. In 'In the Lake Region' the poet has been watching for days the restless movements of a black crow, and hypothesises that 'The ancients would have said her / stubbornness augurs something.' The poem goes on to say:

> The past does not enlighten us – but still, it attempts
> to say something. Perhaps the crow knows more about us
> and about history's dirt than we do ourselves.
> Of what does she want to remind us? Of the black photos, the black headphones
> of radio operators, black signatures under documents,
> of the unarmed with their frozen pupils – of the prisoner's boot or the trunk

of the refugee? Probably not. We will remember this anyway,
though it won't make us any wiser. The bird signifies only stoicism
and patience. If you ask for them, your request will be granted.

Venclova's most recent work offers us a vision of our time and
returns to us fragments of civilisation's aspirations, so often treated
ironically by modern poetry. But Venclova would be the first to
caution us against the belief in any easy solution. One might hear
him saying that the benefits of an outlook such as his might be
small, amounting only to 'stoicism and patience'. But in times
when the recovery of these qualities is paramount, in reading
Venclova's work you may find, if you ask for them, 'your request
will be granted'.

Translating and editing the poems of Tomas Venclova has been a
privilege and a challenge. The completion of this book took several
years and presented a number of considerable obstacles. However,
through close collaboration with the author and Constantine Rusa-
nov, it was possible to establish a successful working method. At
Yale in New Haven, Constantine, a native speaker of Russian,
worked with Tomas on his own translations. In Paris, I was pro-
vided by Constantine with literal versions. I used these to re-
translate the poems from the Lithuanian, in order to establish
strict interlinear versions. For the non-specialist, this means dia-
gramming a poem so that corresponding to each word in the orig-
inal one finds an English equivalent, without any "interpretive"
grammar. This allowed me to understand the logic of word place-
ment and the sense of a line, as well as the relationship of words
to rhyme endings. When this painstaking research proved too
slow, Toma Beinarytè kindly helped me to compile the interlinear
versions. Both my own and Constantine's final versions were read
by Tomas, who answered unending questions regarding words,
personal history and poetics over the indispensable e-mail. The
poems that make up the second part of this book, those by Diana
Senechal, have already appeared in print in the volume *Winter
Dialogue*, published by Northwestern University Press in 1997.

Diana is a Lithuanian speaker and I had the privilege of entering into a dialogue with her on her translations. Based on these reflections, a certain number of the poems presented here are in revised form.

I personally would like to thank Claudia Sinnig in Berlin, German co-translator with Durs Grünbein of Tomas Venclova's poetry (*Gespräche im Winter* [Suhrkamp, 2007]); Mark Carlson and Toma Beinarytė in Paris; in Ireland, Gerard Smyth, for helping at just the right moment, and Kerry Hardie, for her careful reading of the final English manuscript. Constantine Rusanov extends his gratitude to John Hollander and Dale Peterson for their invaluable advice and encouragement. He also wishes to thank the PEN Translation fund for its support of his translations. Above all, Diana, Constantine and I all extend our collective thanks to Tomas Venclova himself, whose inspiring work sustained us.

NOTES

1. Tomas Venclova, *Winter Dialogue*, translated by Diana Senechal (Illinois: Northwestern University Press, 1997), p. xiv. Foreword by Joseph Brodsky.

2. Statistics for this essay were provided by Dr Ceslovas Laurinavicius at the Lithuanian Institute of History in Vilnius. Current research is being carried out to establish ever more exact figures for these events.

3. Tomas Venclova, *Forms of Hope* (Riverdale-on-Hudson: Sheep Meadow Press, 1999), p. 21, 'A Dialogue about a City: Czesław Miłosz and Tomas Venclova'.

4. *Forms of Hope*, p. 138. 'Three Russian Poets'.

The Junction

(2005)

Translations by
ELLEN HINSEY
CONSTANTINE RUSANOV

New England Harbour

Not the sea, but sultry mists, concrete slabs
and discarded rails, pierced by the sunset's sooty carmine
which, from time to time, streaks the sky. Curtained with
fetid algae, the breakwater protrudes – a refuge for seagulls.
Where the sand and strait converge, a figure waits for the crimson
to fade on the far side of the many-masted disorder
and to return home, when the moment comes. But, where is home?
Here, or on the ocean's far shore? In the mountains, where avalanches
have sheared off the slopes? Under back-road firs,
where one can glimpse old cellars' depths? In the ageing body,
which refuses to submit? Or perhaps in the uncertainty
that you have lived? The certainty you will disappear? In this
                              place poisoned by rust –
or again, in the gaze that can still here divine
the symmetry, harmony and measure it manages to find?

[EH]

19

The Émigré

Among more urgent news – briefly, in the phone receiver:
'Didn't you know? A while ago. Alas, she suffered quite a bit.'
I don't know if it was at home. These days, I rarely visit
that deserted zone of shop windows and underpasses.
I don't know the month either. Perhaps it's easier
to pass away in spring: snow's blackening muck,
tree buds stained with coal, puddles – this calms one down,
until one loses interest in resurrection. Alexander,
Edward, Xenia (still alive). A scattered generation.
My memory calls up – a downy cheek, guttural accent, clumsy feet.
Lipstick, too bright. Eyes, not immediately concrete.
In a drawer, a ribbon, receipts and cheques: half a life spent here.

The first three years of exile are wasted –
everyone agrees. Not quite what you'd had in mind:
chilliness in rare letters from home, where neither prison walls,
nor newspaper columns change. Outside the basement window's grating –
ads, antennae, dirt. Near the horizon – the Mormon
Temple's needle spire, like a syringe (heroin, not opium, for the people
Marx would now declare). I can't see it – was she on the train,
or at the steering wheel: all the same, overhead – asphalt,
concrete, scrap metal, a future grave. Elevators complain in darkness.
The dry honeycombs of offices, where your accent
isn't a hindrance, nor does it inspire confidence. Changing continents
doesn't alleviate pain – only death does. To begin, it's worse.

The fact is, so much time has passed. Wrinkles knit by the temple.
Bones are prominent at the wrist – but more so through the fingers.
We knew each other in another life. Spindle trees shone like silver there,

hornbeam groves fell to the valley. There was nothing between us.
Just arguments about friends, poems read. A quarrel once by
a door where two grey-black cement sphinxes, perhaps,
still stand. Later, in the Bronx's better part –
her husband's easel: twisted roots, meant to signify
the enduring link to the motherland, nature, etc. For nature always gets even:
the body overcomes the soul, cells rush the lymph's highway,
the lungs dry, and a doctor utters the Greek word
that offers us up, in sacrifice, to the Brownian law of alkali and acid.

Clouds, damp granite – a grey larynx of water.
These rivers flow nowhere. A raccoon, skulking past the garage
knocks at the door with its snout. A squirrel sputters in the tree's needles.
When I focus on the first street lamp, I almost forget
the darkness. Like an infant's fist, the heart is knocking hard
at what it cannot name. A branch sheds its leaves.
Ants labour. A paint pot flames in the mirror.
Unframed trapezes, hands, stars – dear only to her –
are growing old. It was all long ago.
The shame, the body's degradation, the cough, the body fluid's stench,
the damned desire for the end to come quickly –
and indifferent passersby. Forgive my silence on this end of the line.

[EH]

A New Postcard from the City of K.

Stumbling, foul weather staggers along the Pregel.
Worn pavement, witnessing a fugitive's arrival,
several eternities late, wearily responds.
The landscape shuts its eyes. Only foliage has
kept its Gothic script. The timber frames' cyphers
have become cement blocks. With its tons

of contraband, a train burdens loose crossties.
The Toyotas cloud with their exhaust fumes
the window's ice hole. After some rest,
thanks to a padlock, gates still swing outwards
despite ponderous creaking. Overall, it seems
wisest to avoid the force of their impact.

You once said: if man eternally resorts to revenge,
cities soon tire of their retaliation – to avenge
their ill-treatment with strife, discord.
They forgive everything. Streetcars jingle on
the avenue, where only rails and foundations
recall the sky hailing with shards.

Even if the whole universe returned to dust,
the cars here wouldn't change their routes –
nor the street's networks. But, around
the corner, white concrete panels loom. The park
surrenders to asphalt. And the cathedral's arches
pray to God for a merciful end.

A stalk of wormwood pushes through concrete.
Ragged brick walls conceal the yellow raincoat
of the newcomer, and the mutiny
of several icy gusts of wind encounter a minor
obstacle: a mortal body, which, on this particular
day, happens to be in a foreign country.

Where only air once soared, he sees revolting
vertical shafts. That, is not even talking
about the spirit – it, as the ancients
said, *flat ubi vult*. Still, overgrown ruins and
scattered leaves are better than the standard
grave, which one day we all inherit.

At dusk, from grey neighbourhoods, car fumes
and stench slowly enter the Natangian marshes.
Mantas won, the castle has disappeared.
But, emptiness hasn't surrendered its upper hand:
the sharp quivers of waves shear off the sand –
besieging the shore of Aismares.

The Word, before its inception, returns to dust.
Here, the fierce continental dawn begins to lift
above all hopeless parallelepipeds.
And dreams, after embracing a body like wind,
sweep across the city, where – after time's old
victory – there isn't even room for loss.

Late night. Bomb shards, a century, constellations
press on the roof's tin. In the present configuration
of this wasteland, stripped of its name,
we await morning, as though in a fallout shelter,
not knowing, in the darkness as we lie together,
if we are still ourselves, or someone other.

[EH]

Dunes at Watermill

Some six or seven time zones (I'm not sure
about the exact number) separate
us from the continent, which has by now
turned into post codes and silence. Say,
Long Island: water-polished pebbles, a rough-
hewn wooden pier – the long-familiar view –
a sleepless clear horizon, boats and sails.
The lagoon's elbows touch the barn, the grass.
From here you cannot see the ocean, but
you know it's there: the glimmer of the surf
is barely audible, waves flinging foam
and flakes of jellyfish at footprints (our own
perhaps). The lengthening day wedges into
the door of the garage and leaves a more
permanent mark: the undulating longhand
of tyres which gleams with moisture like a fresh
fingerprint on an application form.
A discontented airplane taints the azure.
Only seagulls are motionless. Commercials
harass the screen, but it has seen far worse.
A shade descends the stairs. Our host attends to
the stove like a witch doctor, dumping out
oysters and shrimp into the boiling water,
his fingers shaky, more than they were last year,
that being the only piece of news on this
island of lotus-eaters.
                              After four
we'll all go to the local bookstore where
his twelve friends will pay tribute to his poems
with humble applause. I never asked him

where he was born. He is not a stranger to
the province I come from (that much I know),
and neither are his listeners, hailing from
adjacent time zones and a common landscape.

Different destinies. Take V., who's sitting
in the far corner, blinded by the sun.
He'll never forget how, many years ago,
he tripped over potholes in the road
as he was running to the station.
Like a mirage, it kept receding further
away and further between walls of concrete.
The consul was no longer on the platform.
He had been fired two days (or hours) before.
But he *was* there, in the compartment, busy.
He leaned out of the train window just
in time to put his clumsy signature
on the life-saving papers and was off.
A different lot fell to A.S., the son
of an attorney (a professor now).
They seized him near the border (a scar marks
the bayonet wound on his shoulder). Later
he rooted out bushes and chopped down trees
in the taiga, becoming an accomplished
lumberjack who did work for two: his mother
didn't have the strength to do men's work. At last,
they fled to freedom through Iran, but that's
another story. The psychiatrist M.
doesn't like to talk about the fetid hole

where he (one of the twenty-seven men
out of five hundred) got away from death.
The guards disbanded and the barbed wire snapped
when a tank rolled into the prison camp.
The strident liberator turned into
a warden before long, but in those days,
thank God, they could still slip away from him,
even those who'd died on more than one occasion.

My friend is driving us back home, his heavy
hand resting on the steering wheel. (Not much
has changed since last year.) He knows more, perhaps,
than all of us. I also come from there.
I didn't fell trees and didn't faint in the barracks,
but I was born there too, in the same time zone.
If continents change, they do so very slowly.
Our retinas must contain identical
imprints, although it may be that where they
had seen a brick wall or a street lamp, I
saw emptiness. I've lived through the last third
part of this century, and yet I've seen
enough of it. But here's the house. We're back.
In front of us, the ivy-covered poles,
the wooden wall smeared with fresh paint all over,
and, on the cool lawn, a newspaper with
new pictures from the Balkan front.

Most likely, nothing else exists besides
these fleeting traces, fragments, imprints on
the sand, the asphalt, on our consciousness,
our passports, and our bodies. The new times
advance like a relentless avalanche
and blot them out. We face old age
and death, which comes at the appointed hour,
like postcards, bills, or an unbidden guest
who interrupts a dinner of shrimp and oysters.

An empty bottle on the table. Night
sweeps up the crumbs and consummates the feast.
The town is nodding off. The motorboats'
lights and the stars commingle in the sky.
A ray of light touches the shelf, and swans
take off for Canada in V-formations.

[CR]

Arrival in Atlantis

On the mud promontory is a ghostly depot.
The sailors don't care what country has capsized,
above all, in these days after a drawn-out
war that's left their empire fragmented.

What is left of the hotel's canteen is the view.
Motorboats list and turn. Coming winter,
framed by curtains, is darker than the window –
veiled by cement and grey-clay spattered.

The red beacon, as before, is solidly squat,
but barely perceptible are the fortress's contours.
Seagulls scuffle on the pier, are more stalwart
than cast iron, concrete: above all, ourselves.

Stand still, close your eyes. A traveller's steps
press into backstreets' sand. Eyesight has failed.
We will never meet again. Wherever one turns
one sees the airless bay and the epoch's end.

Thistle, *Linnaea borealis*, goat weed.
The wet sheen of metal, riddled with holes.
We sense each other, like Almighty God –
from opposite sides of the abyss: far, yet close.

On the sea's threshold where shallows erode,
the darkish strip of the fairway disappears
like black crepe. But under my hands, poverty
November, grammar and flame still flicker.

[EH]

29

For an Older Poet

Snow melted on the balcony. Electric light under the frayed silk shade
cast shadows on the walls. One of them touched
the statue – others, reaching in the opposite direction, tried
to peer out the window. 'Right there – two good lines.'
That's what brought us together. The rest we saw differently:
the weeping willow by the brick wall, terraces of ruddy stones,
summer sand's edge of foam. Yes, I discover within myself
your respect for rhythm, your distrust of formless content.
But I also remember what I wish I didn't: how the distance
between us constantly grew – even while we two
paced out circles around the cold park; even while
we sat in the grass by Naroch Lake, our heads
turned upward, watching how the torn
cartography of clouds unfurls and disintegrates up above.

It wasn't easy. When I was nearly fifteen,
I spied out your weaknesses, the ones you didn't want to own,
or even those of which you were proud. Because of this,
I learned to breathe thin Alpine air, to travel
on the backs of trucks, to light matches in the rain,
to brew bad coffee, to subject myself to self-scrutiny –
all of which, in a way, guaranteed we wouldn't be the same
in voice or script. Nevertheless, you knew more than me:
about the territory beyond the frontier's posts, about the era that circumscribed
our actions like a horizon line; perhaps, even about death (you were
a generation closer), and about language,
which had chosen us both. About syllables, prepositions, stress.
Even today I hear you say: 'fáraway? It must be: farawáy,'
as if one's salvation depended on it. But then, perhaps it does.

You would repeat 'When I'm no longer around,' but you didn't believe it.
Like everyone, you were afraid to disappear. Like others, you hoped
books could at least guarantee a second-rate
immortality. Perhaps you realised that even books could betray you –
when it was too late. You didn't oppose your times.
'How can you blame someone who, at the wheel of his car –
follows the traffic rules?' Of course, there were days
you wished to strike from your consciousness. There were friends
behind barbed wire. You helped some of them – said they
didn't remember the good you'd done. You lived like your contemporaries,
perhaps more consistently – so that I might noiselessly move my lips
repeating the words not said after your departure:
may they rest in peace, Lord. Without nightmares.
And may Eternal Light shine upon them. Like a light in a coal mine.

You rarely appear in dreams these days,
but sometimes you do. We are both hurrying to the station,
stumbling, running late. I stand on the platform, the train
will pull out any second. I must find you,
but I know I won't be able – you are delayed somewhere, the suitcase is heavy,
the corridors are labyrinthine, there are too many steps. But you live on
as long as I follow the echo of your footsteps, your unsteady breathing, the pain
in your chest (which I sometimes also feel). Your gestures continue in me,
no matter how hard I try to suppress them. The cadence of your voice
resurfaces in my foreign speech. As you diminish,
I also grow smaller. One day I'll wake up in the station
and see you. The lamp suspended from the carriage's end
will sway and start to pull away – pick up speed – but we'll remain standing,
without looking at each other, estranged and identical.

[EH]

Two Apocrypha

I

Max Jacob – son of an antiquary – a destitute poet,
who had been trying all his life to find
two or three words that would contain the universe,
was better known for his top hat, monocle and horoscopes,
which often turned out to be true.
                              A city slicker, friend
of Guillaume and Pablo, he felt that time was tantamount
to disaster, while bridges, cupolas, white shutters, boulevards,
plane trees in winter, unconscious of their own beauty,
and, finally, himself –
were but decoration. What lies beyond
will one day sweep it all away. Laws break down, and everything
returns to the primordial gloom. He was haunted by dreams
of being chased, now by werewolves, now by police dogs.
He hid in a dustbin, knowing that he would wake up
in a cold operating-room to the soft clinking of lancets.

I don't know if the dusty cinema hall has been preserved
(was it rue Ravignan? Rue du Cherche Midi?),
where – after the battle of the Marne – the Virgin appeared before him.
In the middle of a silent film noir, she addressed him from the screen
in obscene Parisian argot, for it was unlikely that he would
have understood any other language. After that,
Max Jacob lived for thirty more years.
He tried many times to dismiss that voice, shielding himself
with fashion, irony, masks, with the childish passion to excel.
But one day he wrote down the words that neither Luke nor John attests to,
the words that might have been uttered by the Virgin herself:

God exists, and this is unthinkable.
God does not die, and this is unthinkable.
God has a forehead, a mouth, a bed, a mother, and this is unthinkable.

In the end, he was overtaken by the dogs and the lancets.
In the camp at Drancy, on a plank bed, having lost
his monocle, the cupolas, the bridges,
his friends and relatives, himself, he probably realised
that these words would suffice.

II

N.N., a private soldier,
at about the same time when the poet died in Drancy,
was in a different camp, on the other side of another front.
He was spared the pit filled with the rotting bodies of officers
shot in the back of the head. The fate of privates
is always simpler: hunger, lice, illness.
In the barracks, he had visions of a sludgy shallow river,
of haystacks on the bank. Then – of a ruined anthill
beneath spruce trunks and needles. The private realised
that what he saw was a hallucination, as the dark
inrush of fever would destroy at once the imaginary world.
He had neither cigarettes, nor water, let alone vodka.
It would have been difficult even to swallow. But that is not
the worst thing. A stench hovers over the bunk beds.
It seems that no one is any longer capable of getting up
or cares any more. He alone crawls toward the ditch in order

to squat on a transverse log (once you fall down – it's all over).
                                        It was there,
N.N. told me many years later, that the Virgin had appeared before him.

Without the wax, the incense, the altar, the icons and the offerings,
she was the same as ever. She said: 'Tomorrow you'll be free.'
No one knows why she chose him and not somebody else.
He was a ribald and a libertine. He hardly ever prayed, even
in the barracks, where other inmates would assemble crosses
out of woodchips. They were all let go in the morning.
Amnesty followed the treaty.

He alone remained in the camp for another half a year: as usual,
misplaced papers, mixed-up family names, a missing date of birth.
But he was already free. Free until this very day.

One cannot comprehend what all this means. So many friends
have died. What remains are mystery and patience, bread and wine.

[CR]

The Junction

From the highway, down to the meadow
led the path. In the ravine, you watched
the sunset brush up against wires, fade.
The State's mark crowned the signpost
and bittercress stems scratched cement.

A country, long-suffering and patient,
lay to the north-east welcoming night.
A doe nibbled brushwood and alder.
Beyond the horizon, you could almost
see a distant lake. In its clouded surface
was the indistinct reflection of a child
whose outline matched yours. Above,
a song hovered over the bridge and
rushes, on mossy tombstones' dates.
Time that escapes biographers and
memory is perhaps the most important:
both a heavy burden and a talisman.

To the left stretched the wild wood.
In it, a bright opening – a gap which
revealed a marsh, or simply mud or silt.
There, unseen, swarmed the grinning,
unkempt offspring of absurd designs
and schemes. In the distance ruined
bridges and glades showed black. Icy
canals took aim at the cold fringes
of the bay, but failed to hit the city
or the fleet. You know that children
there are born into side streets sharing
rage, cigarette butts, sperm, syringes.

Whitish chimney smoke behind you,
and growling dogs that keep guard
against unwelcome guests. It's late.
Impassable dirt roads wind round
past hollows and debris. Unplastered
brick walls conceal the fires. I guess
if fate has brought you here, you should
accept this territory at the threshold
of home. This triple-junction strewn
with rigid signposts – now outdated,
but one time deadly. The viaduct's
grim arch spans neglected grounds.

Touch the cold grass of childhood.
You are home. Night's shell enfolds
the three-fold sea. It's all a gift of grace:
these muddled times, the sentry no longer
on guard, the air that's longing for a voice.

[EH]

After the Lecture

That day, as usual, we were reading verse,
composed in a language that my students
had not quite mastered.
                    Puddles outside
were glistening, and the walls were shot with grey.
The unemployed had built them in the time
of the depression, and the style is known
appropriately as *Depression Gothic*.
I had a feeling that my words weren't apt
and missed the mark. My voice disobeyed me.
The chalk was crumbling in my hand, and all,
it seemed, was somewhat dreamlike and unreal.
With little success, I was attempting to explain
what then I deemed important (and still do):
that consonants catch sight of their kin
and call to one another, not unlike
stray hunters – softly, nonetheless distinctly;
that vowels move up and down the scale;
that syllables reduplicate themselves
like mirrors, contraposed to produce
vertiginous and darkling enfilades,
wherein the stress recedes, reflected like a candle.
A series, in short, of more or less
banal comparisons – for them to realise
that nothing in a line of verse is trivial;
the more minute a grain of sand, the more
perceptibly it may affect the current.
Besides, poetic lines contain enigmas
dictated by the very sound scale:

forbidden names of godhead, which have come
to stand for ordinary objects, words
that are significant, though unassuming,
like talismans. The whirlwind above
the stanza is called metaphor. It bends
the phrase down like the grass and shuffles sounds
like clouds, until remote, though at heart
related, meanings meet, and their union
is by the lexicon pronounced holy.

The students were packing their books,
and I fell silent, while the world was changing.
The panes were, as before, reflecting puddles
and cheerless turrets jutting out above.
A room was showing through them, however –
in a remote country that no longer
existed – and a portly woman, whom I
had known, was in it, sinking in an armchair.
Yet she was strangely elegant. I feared
her biting words, her memory that compassed
a great deal more than my own age and time,
but, as we both were going up the stairs,
I feared even more that she
might suddenly stop breathing. She was silent,
but, possibly, I knew what she was thinking.

This is, indeed, the truth, though one could put it
more plainly. There's no point in denying
that this is part of our task and calling.

It will suffice to heed and follow language,
allowing it to lead you on – it will
supply you with the tone, the rhythm; perhaps,
with anagram and metaphor as well.
But poetry comes into being before
we do and even before language. It arises
first in the soundless realm of nothingness.
A poem rests and dreams about itself,
and our task is to disturb these dreams,
to lead it out of them – out of the void –
into the streets of syntax and of sound.
But this requires assistance, I suspect,
of someone yet more powerful than language.
If Saint Augustine is to be believed –
but, to be sure, he spoke the truth – the Lord
forever treasures up within Himself
all rivers, dawns, and sunsets, every tear
and every atom, every meagre ration
a prisoner devours and every bullet.
This is too much for us, and we make do
with fragments: say, a heron on the coast,
an awkward arch, *Depression Gothic* style,
or weeds beneath the balcony, which was
inscribed of old with gilded letters: *Deus
conservat omnia*. But that's sufficient
for poems to contain our love in its
entirety, for them to comfort both
the living and the dead.

Let's honour language,
its appositions, mazes, interchanges,
which almost make it possible for us
to measure up to God. Not quite, of course,
since there still lies ahead of us a wall
that we cannot step over. Language will
cease to exist, like we all do, but this
is poor grounds for irony.
                    Outside
I saw the ice-cold otherworldly sky.
It was late March.

[CR]

Užupis

Under an uproar of lindens, before the stone
embankment, by a fast current like the Tiber,
I am drinking Gilbey's with two bearded men.
In the twilight – the jingle of glasses, smoke.
But we have never met. I knew their parents.

Generations overtake another. The tape-recorder
warbles and crackles. My two interlocutors
want to know about questions I once pondered:
whether there is meaning to suffering and mercy –
whether art can survive if it obeys no rules.

I was the same as them, but destiny accorded
me a strange fate: this, of course, is no better
than any other. I know evil never disappears,
but one can at least strive to dispel blindness –
and poetry is more meaningful than dreams.

In summertime, I often wake before dawn,
sensing, without fear, the time is drawing
close when others will inherit the dictionary,
along with clouds, ruins, salt and bread.
And freedom is all that I will be granted.

[EH]

Theseus Leaving Athens

An old man sits down on the sand beside the town gates.
The dusk arrives in Athens earlier than in Crete.
Thickening shadows cling to the feet resembling,
in their last agony, the Minotaur, whose entrails
have been cut open by bronze. The monstrous offspring
of a crowned whore made pregnant by a bull, it thrived on
the blood of virgins, scattering the waste all over
the labyrinth, where, struck down by the sword, it perished
at last. Some think the bull was one of the many shapes
Poseidon took, from which it follows that two brothers
were fighting, since the victor also was begotten
by the ferocious sea god. In the granite cave, our hero
suddenly realised this, as the maze unwound
in twists and turns much like the thread that singed his palm.
All those he killed, including monsters, were brothers.

Old age condenses space and glues it up like resin.
Out in the distance he sees hills, once sharp, now blunted
by time, which he passed on the way from Troezen to
the far-famed city that belonged to him by right.
Like Tantalus (one of his ancestors), he thirsted
for the whole universe: the olive grove, the laurel,
the vineyard and the press, the slabs of marble forming
a dreary arid precipice, the tetrahedral
unfinished rough-walled temples, and the splendid chariot
the red-haired Phoebus drives above the deep blue sea.
Fair women's bodies showing through translucent clothes,
the down of private parts submitting to his touch...
When he wakes up, his heavy eyelids stick together.
He took the longest byway, jubilantly clearing
the land of the accursed seed of wolves and serpents.

They were his brothers also, including Procrustes.
Old age, odd as it sounds, is like Procrustes' bed.
Your destiny fails to contain you but surpasses
your dwindling strength. Strange dreams recur, which are more vivid
than memory. Most often, those involving anguish.
Somebody leaves the palace never to return.
One hears no sound of steps. A rustling peplos. Is it
Queen Phaedra who embraced the black glare of her loss?
Her sister, handed over to a frenzied god?
Persephone? He once descended to her kingdom,
but all he saw were reeds and woodlice, slugs and snails,
slippery subterranean slopes and wandering souls.
One day, perhaps, among them he'll catch sight of Phaedra
and of his son, whose head was crushed by horses' hooves,
though shades hardly ever recognise each other.

A sailboat struggles with the wind near Salamis.
The gods play dice, and mortals must be satisfied with
remorse, forgiveness, the desire to understand.
He came to terms with bitter fate. He decorated
the city and paid tribute to the dead. He welcomed
the blinded foreign king. Panathenean torches burn
at his behest. And even as he dies, new temples,
new monuments and gardens will spring up. But they
will also vanish. Now and then he hears
a voice that's greater than the voice of God, declaring:
'You did your best.' Reposing at the gates of Athens,
he came to comprehend the meaning of these words.
All that was bound to happen – came to pass, and shortly
Lycomedes will push him off the cliff, just as
some time ago he'd done the same to Sciron.

[CR]

On a Mountain Ridge Near Jordan

This is not a mountain, but a wasteland's
precipice. Before the daunting height,
afraid, you soar above the plain like a
formless angel. Sensations deceive you:
though my eyes are sharp-sighted as before,
and my strength is firm, I cannot trespass
this threshold. What to the Lord is but a
fine thread – and for others, a rivulet –
for me is a sign of abyss and fate.
My tongue stumbles as it once did in youth.
The still-proud walls of Jericho wedge
into the valley. On the rim of an azure
basin: the poisoned, salt land of Sodom,
and to the north, the air shimmers over
Lake Tiberias' invisible sea.
Near the horizon, I prophesy a city –
a land of ruins, longing and discord.
It does not yet stand. White ravines shine there,
as well as a hill – the shape of a skull,
which seems to speak of events to come.

I have never seen the Promised Land.
Sired on foreign soil, with an alien name,
I heard it from an elderly wet nurse
(perhaps my very mother) who was born
as well to a house of bondage, beneath
the rough-stepped incline of the pyramids.
I will always be between two countries.
I barely remember the first one where

the slave-driver's merciless lash rang out,
and where dried blood gathers in the corners
of the mouth. It still comes to me in dreams,
but then I awake, so as not to yearn
for that lost kingdom of the dead, Sheol.
The spring that rises up from Midian's land
is better – there, I tended sheep and chose
for my son the name of 'foreigner'.
Then, cruel cities were flooded by darkness,
the heavens split, the sea was rent in two –
I don't recall much more. To tell the truth,
this arid wilderness is all I know.

It is eternal. One soon gets used to
it, as if it were time and space itself.
At midnight, a host of pitiless stars
watch a lonely nomad from heaven's vault.
On the horizon dry, black mountains stand.
Wind's millstones grind earth back into its grains,
for it doesn't care what it devours –
camels' bones, or our own. Israel's twelve tribes
dissolve in this wide, open expanse like
salt in a brook. But the waters are locked
in the depth of the rock. Baal-Zebub
reigns here supreme: emptiness,
Master of pride, strife and treason.
God endows this wasted land with heat
and thirst, the way he fills grapes with sweetness.
White hailstones injure the mouth, but there is
no other nourishment to hand. Only today,

after so many years, we have reached
the steep cliff where I shall die. Palm leaves rustle,
and a pale flame pulses where we have paused.

Its movements, I believe, are life itself.
Neither the keystone of the temple nor
the copper sea contain the flame that once
brought the burning bush to its flowering,
while someone spoke to me the great, 'I Am' –
for it is but these words alone that may
define Him. He was without others when
He spoke to me, without the seraphim;
shining forth from a mountain ridge He split
the ground, a thunderbolt clasped in His right
hand. At night, He was a blazing pillar
of fire: the guide whose glory is ineffable.
Destroyer and enlightener, unexpectedness –
at once, black thunder, questions, anguish,
and change – though one can't tell what is changing.
Dry grass, I am consumed by the fire that
destroys us, the tents, the constellations,
and suddenly severs the connection
between son and father, past and future,
for the universe is part of this flame.

Afraid, I tried to hide myself from Him –
in forms of wisdom, tables and taboos.
The imperative commands, etched in stone,
will be disobeyed by near everyone,
but even for this, they must still exist.

I didn't possess the will to bear
the burden when, days past, we camped near Marib.
But these are just ashes of a bonfire,
wood's charred remains whose blackness is pierced
by fire, so that it might blaze up again.
The sum of all moments creates the soul,
as grains of sand, a desert. By the cliff's
side, I am the same: one who fire awoke,
who spurned the damnation of the Nile,
who understood that perseverance must
precede rest, fatigue – reward, homeland,
by lone hours in the desert, age before those
not yet conceived, who will never long for
Egypt: for here by the bonfire's embers
there dwells the spirit that once spoke to me.

[EH]

Discipline and Punish. A Visit to the Detention Centre IZ-45/1

And I pray not for myself alone...
ANNA AKHMATOVA

It's easier to survive in here than before.
Problems are the same outside: AIDS, TB.
Bromine mixed in gruel somewhat quells
sperm's rage, when outside one happens
to see the contours of female visitors' calves,
as the guards are indulging in Baltika beer.

Words no longer mean the same, the town
roars – divided into two, near the red wall.
A cluster of clouds, a continent behind your
back. When the wind lifts they say a paper
scrap sometimes reaches the other shore,

though more often falls on passing barges –
or simply, onto the flickering ultramarine.
Still, a sign to the morning, algae, nature.
In a cell: six men, not twenty, as before.

A church dome. Beyond, a streetcar's route.
The blind brick wall has learned the slang
of skinheads. Was it far in those days – ?
From neglected gardens, decaying columns
down the avenue, disfigured by modernity,

over the bridge's desert, along two streets.
July heat. The deafening rustle of leaves –
blood beats in the veins at a regular rate.
It has been years since the silhouettes of
friends or enemies showed in windowpanes.

Clearings, empty spaces. An émigré felled
on stage in Berlin by a madman's bullet,
leaving behind a son: an uncommon destiny.
A proud, nearsighted poet (whose memory
will be preserved in a field near Magadan);

even the other, who would be born later –
the long road and the polar night over
the Yenisei prepare themselves for him,
(and the Neva and Neman and the river
without a name in Charon's kingdom).

And others who were sure there existed
unfettered air and another life. Here it is:
beyond the gates sparrows scurry about.
A steam boat bellows. We inherit the earth.
Though this is probably small consolation.

[EH]

From Landwehrkanal to Spree

(for Murat Khadzhu)

An outcast, God knows how long ago,
I drank the viscous honey and the gall
of exile here, as I was playing tarot
or, on occasion, chess with providence.
Impersonating Ovid, I looked on
the ranks of half-abandoned houses, run
and guarded by a *Stasi* garrison
that billeted across the lethal fence.

The old canal, where Rosa had been found,
reflected ruins. It is no longer bound
to do so. Railway stations come around.
Has anything at all escaped the flux?
A flame extends the alleyway, or rather,
spouts out of it, like egg-white, toward ether.
The flags of yesteryear's colossi wither
above the embassies. *Pariser Platz.*

I watch the desolate postmodern era
that dwells between the bar and parking area
near the bank, whose atrium is more sterile
than the Sahara or the dried-up Nile.
My gaze pursues the shimmering rails
to where they intersect, threadlike and frail,
upon the spot where the *Siegessäule* nails
the sky in resolute denial.

The Wall that once epitomised the Styx
has vanished, disassembled into bricks.
The princedom of consumerism and sex
won't solve the riddles of the tourist
who may be on the lookout for the past.
The Politburo's seat has been recast
to house the work of an avant-gardist
who'd fled the country that ceased to exist.

Inebriate of freedom, he and I
are out-of-place, anachronistic like
two Huguenots. But I am still alive,
for good or bad, and holding forth onstage.
Having experienced both heat and cold,
I stand beneath the bridge's faceless vault,
surrounded by granite and basalt,
in a bewildering new-fangled age

to which I don't belong, like Hercules
upon the pediment, his chariot, his cuirass,
which were baptised by fire and en masse
thrown up into the present by the tide
of the deluge. So long as they resist
the onrush of the chilly April breeze,
Athena, patroness of cities, is
my only goddess and my only guide.

One, I would say, is always a newcomer
in her domain, where empires come and
go, and epochs, ridiculed, flash by like comets,
inconstant like the lure and charm of triumph.
Robbed of his name, his native land, his hearth,
a man adapts to solitude and dearth
and is (an émigré once said) immersed
in time like the salamander is in fire.

This is, perhaps, the only gift of grace
in a terrain where the word '*ohne*' reigns.
Hang on until your journey ends, embrace
the flame. No one will help you with advice.
Dust-heaps are brimming with ideas and lies.
Though you were frail and paltry, you despised
untruth and bondage, fearing danger less
than chains, and were prepared to pay the price.

An angel hovers overhead. It may
bring good or evil. Be it either way,
I'm late for our rendezvous today,
but, all the same, I wish to thank my fate.
The constellations haven't yet set in.
I wend my way to where the Wall had been
and disappear, having erased my twin
from the storefront to set my record straight.

[CR]

Ormond Quay

(for Seamus Heaney)

The ocean mist, amassing in April above Dublin,
moistens bricks, granite, the pitch-black of a car's
sheen. The tide-abandoned riverbed is silty, lays
bare an expanse beneath bridges, empty like an

open palm. This muddy island has known famine,
mutiny. Twenty years ago was shallow as the Liffey,
but now, waking at dawn to the groan of the lorries,
the river's high mark has once again been regained –

or surpassed. A wailing seagull flies into a breach
between warehouses. Pavements are cracked, damp.
By the tower, the bay whispers through raindrops,
branches, time. But it's not us who taught it speech.

Bronze by gold. The staircases are steep, bread bitter,
but the pay sustains. On the quay's corner you sight
the famous siren's den, fully packed, where a migrant
poet drinks to his double's reflection across the bar.

It's all the same. The brown of northern marshes; the
Ionian shore's blue towards which one wearies of rowing.
Like Circe's bed the old rumpled map is expanding:
homeless Europe buries itself in a coarse-grained sheet.

[EH]

Song of the Borderland

As you near the frontier, the dunes are steeper.
Boulders with rusty lichens of yellow and green.
Later, a thunderstorm will drain them of colour
as in the tropics: the earth left stunned by rain.
The wind's embrace wrinkles air; shines conifer's
needles. The lacklustre lake's ellipsis opens on
a layer of silt, and the dark over paths fractures
into parts as, under an icy torch, the skin burns.
Nearer the edge, lightning's flashes are fainter –
the sky widens. Thunderclouds erode. Undone,
the heart chases the clock. In your old manner
of saying, rejoices knowing the clock will win.

Get used to twilight, let silence teach you to hear.
A highway's dip holds a chaos of stones and rain.
By the roadside a puddle boils with alkalic silver,
bindweed holds quartz, feldspar and mica joined.
The orchestra's polyphony drowns in the *do*'s roar –
soundlessly, the burning bush fades. Mountain
ridges choke with mud. The moraine's rising water
parches the larynx. Blindness flares in the retina's
depth. Get used to night vision, hear the unheard
in sound's scale. Engines drone on, half-drowned
in expanding Lethe. The headlights are off. Stare
hard in the dark to find the hornbeam's skeleton.

The close room is chaotic as the end draws near –
like cumulus undone by explosion. Curtains turn
to vapour in the window's ice-hole. Bent banisters
loom where the door should be. It's hard to discern
the cassette's slow, tapering sound. By the door's
open bolt, the chrome of the faucet dully shines.
Between purulent glass and the eyelids of shutters,
slivers of light enter and seek their refuge within.
Darker the nameless notes, the nearer the stars.
Emptiness will take all that music turns to stone.
Like a sail over sleeplessness floats death's hour:
after breathing ends, the tape will continue to spin.

Set your gaze to the interval, loss will sharpen your
hearing. Listen to the slack voices: you may learn
to feel at home when the colourless, formless future
invades you. A future without lightning, rain, ruins.
Voice has vanished, but the Echo, far from hearing,
blooms like a rosebush in waste, in the dark goes on.
About piano keys or windowpanes: it doesn't care –
nor about the borderland blindly embraced by night.
Train your sight to absence, your intrinsic harbour.
Hear the Echo lift from the woods, constellations,
the airless space and indifferent nature – it never
needed the universe, nor the spheres, as they turn.

[EH]

Homage to Shqiperia

Survey the amphitheatre's ruined hemisphere,
the rocky semicircle – its spokes like pauses
in a monologue. The stage is nearly ideal.
The sponger from the cleverest comedy by Plautus
waves his hand at us. Once Epidamnos was here –
in this poor country, now excessively real.

Our memento: a paper entry, thumbed threadbare,
with a mountain's contour, two words: *pesë lekë*,
and a black locomotive that seems to exist only
on bills. And the rest – windows gaping empty,
rank straw on pavement, the shadow of a bunker
by the coarse, red-haired spine of a donkey.

Phlegethon blazes up in a leeward hollow,
where armed, naked slopes pound water's reflection.
If one were to imagine Europe as a solar system
(oscillating planets, harmonic bonds of constellations),
this country would then be scorching Pluto
whose position is silence and abandon.

One would rather be where one is not, again
I recall this proverb. Here, pomegranates aren't mature,
but the grenades are overripe. I have outlived
three dictators. From exile's safe distance, three more.
But this local version was far worse than
the others combined. I'd even say he slammed

the door shut to the otherworld. Glass grinds
underfoot. A machine gun's slit is like a rotten socket
in a Martian's skull. Networks of bunkers were
dug in limestone, as if posterity needed to be instructed
that there would never again be hell or paradise,
air or water, but only, and at best, fire.

Near sunset, against its will, smell's keen faculty
detects the odour of rats, rubbish, rakia.
Under a veil of ash, a constellation starts to stir –
the way dead white acanthus leaves shake,
the way emptiness drones! It draws its weight from bodies
and then ripens slowly in the atmosphere.

On the dry marble, fruit rinds glow white,
and the ancient comic's contour faintly appears
in tobacco smoke. In my sleep, I hear declaimed:
'*Panta rhei* comes to where stagnation was before –
as to which is better, not even God can predict.
It's a dollar for the wine – two for the aphorism.'

[EH]

Anno Domini 2002

A homeless star overhead: a sign of winter and miracle.
The city, like an airplane, descends into New Year's
bright unknown. Global warming's virus makes the towers
shiver. The flat archipelago wheezes and coughs.
The white statue – the chess queen – has lost her

place: hopelessly entangled in a knotted web of drizzle.
The Rubicon was crossed by the Cimbri – or ourselves.
The horizon's arc: Venetian-blind sharp, a half-closed eye.
A drop dilates the pupil, precipitation fogs the larynx.
By the corner, scaffolding rises, an empty cinema glows,

and you descend stairs into the weekend's thick prose.
You won't see the Latin *Salve* on the worn-out threshold –
this is not your home. Parquet sags, fractures like ice
under exile's feet. A new Jugendstil panel is sacrificed
to clients, unwillingly, in its glory: pink and lilac-toned

above the bar. Tablecloths' sails, mirrors, bronze, crystal,
fake marble. Yes – on this very same Fifty-Second Street
(how did the poet put it?) you are sitting uncertain, afraid,
over a glass of wine, while an occasional dirty snowflake
marks the era like a cross, which at a rapid rate retreats

into the Mesozoic Age. Death's odour, unmentionable,
offends the September, October, November, December
night – one loses count. It hovers a hundred blocks away
hanging over pride and ash (though neither remains) –
along with iron heaps: twisted into ribbons and cinder.

Fire sets us back to the beginning. War alas, is primal,
peace, secondary. Water's older than earth. There's ice
enough in the Arctic to cover, if not the world's surface,
then at least this granite island. And less oil suffices –
for a tower, a man – muscles, skin and the eye's iris.

Somewhere on a makeshift bed, in a tent, head cradled
by a fist, a young man dreams of glory games, airplanes –
fire. We alone have created him. For him there is only
this destiny. Now it is time for us to pay. Through the
smoke, a subway token rolls across the floor, jingles

like a sestertius coin into the lava of Herculaneum.

[EH]

La Baigneuse

It's difficult to say now what exactly happened –
but on a narrow embankment I am illuminated
by the silvery radiances of water – splintering.
A boat tears the canal like a dull ploughshare,
and from bridges to the speckled roofs there
lies the city laid open: a fruit which is splitting

on sullied glass. Freshwater ripples (or perhaps
silence) stubbornly batter the hulls of ships.
A moving shadow crosses over the unsigned
canvas of the bay. Blue cloths hang slantwise
down bricks grown thick with lichen. Colours
darken. On the retina: Guardi's visions of wind.

Calli, campi, campielli. Long blackened stone.
On old arches: the lagoon's damp inscriptions.
The sky is right out of another century. Crazy
Clio overlooked these walls, which now only
face the threat of silt, rising tides and gravity.
Foundations revert to the peaceful element, the

city wades in space. You drift, up to your knees
in the tepid spume of marble façades, or the sea –
which gives off a stink of machine oil and rot.
While almost beyond vision's grasp, overhead,
is the white lion, with his wisest of books, filled
with pity for the living and the dead. For it's not

we, but he alone, who knows the final verdict –
to which the eternal race of seconds submits,
including all forms, from angels to trilobites:
even the facing of the pediment, now crumbing,
or the island, where grass covers bones waiting
for the final morning of God that never comes.

The sirocco tears up the wall's lace. Sultriness
covers up the face with a mask (though there's
no face), darkens cupola scales and the copper
of weather vanes. The city slowly floats towards
the deep primeval kingdom of slippery creatures –
flounder, electric-ray, sea squirts, *frutti di mare*.

Towards evening – a glass of wine in the café.
On the square's far side, a monochrome, rough
abyss. But the eye makes peace with the dim
sea thanks to the multifaceted cathedral: a chest
for dowry. Sledge-hammers shake its vault, but
our hands entwine, outweighing pain and time.

[EH]

On the Boulevard by Town Hall

You are indistinct, but the setting's explicit:
gas-meters, coal fumes, the narrow kitchen's
stench, cracked pavements, sparrow fleets,
the baroque bedecked in clouds and pigeons.

Here, almost a half-century ago, I entered
the universe you had managed to fashion
out of rare, leftover scraps of childhood –
bas-reliefs, cushions, poverty and porcelain.

My hand once sought your rustling clothes.
I stared past the gaunt skin reflecting upon
the floral tablecloth. Even then, the peonies
foretold your future: the abandoned garden

that you now inhabit. Others sit in the cafés.
For them, our century's shorter than a minute.
The boulevard is clear, and the future's arrived –
when it shouldn't have. You're no longer in it.

[EH]

A Valediction, Forbidding Mourning

Our morning rooms filled with jasmine and dust.
The window, like a screen, cut off by arches from
the murky canal, contained passersbys' backs, lime-
spattered gateways, the poplar's oblong rhombus,

at times, your raincoat. Those passé fashions out
of the Thaw. When you were late, I felt robbed
of the gift of speech. For four years we parted
or, to put it more truthfully, right from the start.

No Tristan in search of a sail: an astronomer
perhaps, clinging to his lens in the Alpine night,
I spied, by the crossroads, the yellow, soot-coated
house. And later, a slender figure drawing near.

The courtyards were destroyed. Only the canal
and streets' telescopes endure. When I happen
here (on either way to the terminal) I can even
see the dead in the streets' depth, but have little

hope of seeing you. Little desire. If, when I halt,
blood presses on the aorta, it doesn't really last.
Just as slow-moving planets in orbital paths pass,
only the tide registers the gravitation, barely felt.

A poet would have said only enjambment endures.
Words, once near to each other, return to the void –
a line or stanza breaks from another. Though poor
syntax tries to unite what the rhyme has severed.

[EH]

63

Commentary

Above all, though it's hard, love language –
humbled in newspapers, obituaries saturated with lies,
in the bedroom's close darkness, the informer's confession,
in the cry at the bazaar, trenches, the stench of hospital wards,

in third-rate theatres, secret police offices, on lavatory walls.
In grey buildings where the stairwell's shaft is guarded
by steel nets, so that it is not a man, but the century,
which selects the instant of his death;

this language, almost collapsed, littered with sound
and fury. That's it, love language –
banished to earth beside us,
though carrying with it the primordial Word,

as if conceived in that other universe.
It was given so that we might be different from clay,
the palm, the thrush, perhaps even from angels,
so that by naming, we should grasp objects clearly.

Those who attempt to return to that untouchable realm,
to purify their language, must understand
that failure will be their lot. Because perception
up there recedes as quickly as one approaches –

and insight is equal to loss: what is formed
is as quickly effaced. And don't trespass
into another's heaven (there are many). To reach
any heaven is to erase your footprints and discard the key.

They say you are only a tool. Dictated to by
a force you can't face head-on or you'll go blind.
That's not entirely true. Gropingly, you'll climb Jacob's ladder
in a dream, exceeding your strength, unprotected by a net,

until, above, someone greets you (or perhaps doesn't). Still,
sometimes, casting you aside, he might transpose a word
or two, change a vowel, tighten syntax, shift a degree.
This happens rarely, but it does happen –

then you'll be the one who 'saw that it was good' –
because letters float across the page like sludge on a river,
and suddenly bushes, an embankment, a city come into view.
And it doesn't matter who reads this (if anyone ever).

[EH]

In the Lake Region

When you open the door, everything falls into place –
the little ferry by the wharf, fir trees and thujas.
An old woman, feeding ducks, seems as old as Leni
Riefenstahl. At the base of the hill, chestnut trees, not yet in full bloom,
are younger – but probably as old as her films.
All is wet and bright. A hedgehog or God-knows-whose-soul
is rummaging in last year's leaves. Dead water and living water
fill the plain. The twins Celsius and Fahrenheit
are predicting spring weather – while a shadow obscures
the past (just like the present). The first serene weeks scour the bridges
in a peaceful corner of Europe between Wannsee and Potsdam – where
much has happened, but, probably, nothing more will.
For days we have been watching a ragged crow – in the garden,
sometimes on the roof. The ancients would have said her
stubbornness augurs something. Emerging from the wood's
depths, she lights on one antenna crossbar
then another, her surface bright as mercury
in a thermometer's glass. But these are fever marks
we are incapable of understanding. The beginning of agony?
The past does not enlighten us – but still, it attempts
to say something. Perhaps the crow knows more about us
and about history's dirt than we do ourselves.
Of what does she want to remind us? Of the black photos, the black headphones
of radio operators, black signatures under documents,
of the unarmed with their frozen pupils – of the prisoner's boot or the trunk
of the refugee? Probably not. We will remember this anyway,
though it won't make us any wiser. The bird signifies only stoicism
and patience. If you ask for them, your request will be granted.

[EH]

Limbo

At half past seven,
the square awakens, lightens –
a cloud's shadow and the sun
chase each other across flagstones,
turn them into a map of being,
and non-being; the chairs
of a nearby café climb one upon
the other, like Pelion on Ossa,
and slate-coloured doves
draw circles between arcades and stone masks,
but never reach the towers
crowned with tiara and bonnet
(and, a bit further, like a cap that's
been dropped, a small church protrudes).
Umbrella sails fly – a commercial harbour.
A statue twists upward, a tongue of flame.

At half past seven,
stones tumble like dice,
acacias rustle – a wing
parses Latin to the wind,
and a triumphant droplet
disturbs the fountain's pliant
surface. Intermittently, you hear:
now, a camera's click, then, a cell phone
ringing nearby, in a curtained hall
filled with city maps from the last century,
(towers, stations, official buildings).
Bicycle tyres try to navigate the convex surface of the square,
and a long monologue of bells ripens
without punctuation marks.

The air is generous and cold.
Mirrors alone are reliable – above all, when they reflect
nothing. Or at most, a line of type, hanging upside down
(desert ambush, hostage crisis,
another secret factory,
the dictator loves football, forbidden for his subjects),
all easily covered over, by turning the page.

At half-past seven,
in this, the most peaceful of the circles set aside for us,
umbrellas squeak over wet tables,
a light's ray under a tree falls
on necklace and brooch,
a load of sugar weighs down
the freckled snowdrift of a cappuccino,
fingers trace the tablecloth, turpentine
is caught in the thuja's armour,
and time grows – alien, progressively heavy,
becomes itself without our
will or knowledge. The clock's dark hand
counts out its fractions, and the little orchestra
on the tilting deck plays on.

[EH]

He Who Turned Around at the Border
(for M.K.)

The path to be climbed was strewn with debris –
up from an underground beyond comprehension:
perilous chasms, parched yellow clay and dread,
hieroglyphics of crags and dark-haired woods,
rising from grey twilight like a drowned man.
Until the wanderer felt he no longer knew his

way: there, where a soul, falling asleep, wastes,
far from terrestrial fields. Still, music swelled in
his mind: that power to which Hades submits,
and which precedes all, brought into being out
of nothingness; which reigns over hyperborean
ice and the Nile's heat – for it alone possesses

meaning. As the music receded to the depths,
the more to him it sounded: discernable barely
beneath the stone vault where Chronos pauses
from destruction. It promised return from those
mirrors that hold no trace, able to free a body
from its poison, or clothe again its emptiness

with form, so it might endure. Far off he heard,
it seemed, a shade's slow steps. Brushing cold sweat
from his brow, he sacrificed Terpander and Sappho
not yet born, for the promise of his companion –
the slight mark on her cheek, her transparent
locks of hair... and if her muscles were ragged,

would her smile still remain? The keen thirst
that pressed him on, urged him to turn around.
Was she the same? Would she still remember,
or wish for the unfortunate weight of desire –
destiny, future, herself? If not, then his end
would be Thrace's night, its flutes and Bacchantes.

He glanced back. The world had disappeared,
the landscape all but dissolved. The timid cries
of seagulls rose and Eurus lashed the wild
slope – bent like a lyre's string by the wind.
The crags vanished. Far above were white stars.
There to greet, centuries later, the *Inferno*'s bard.

[EH]

Antonio Vivaldi
(for T.M.)

A light ray's solo subdues the choir of seconds.
Like a sign manifest, this day is resolutely over:
beyond roofs' sloping tin and asbestos, the pier
is battered by spray, nearly autumnal, weightless.

Beyond the city, another August sun retreats.
A shabby, grey portal is destroyed by moisture.
Pilasters cool. But *Se parto, se resto* continues,
growing under a glass roof, as in Eden's thickets.

Like a cicada in the realm of a musical wood,
the mantle's statuette drowns in a string's echo,
turns into a voice itself, as if sensing it must go –
since bodies never leave any trace in the sand.

Reaching the speed of angels, it dances, pirouettes.
Grasps a sharp above the dense forest of notes:
dissolves in air. The time has come for farewells.
It's dark. And to be thankful for: there's nothing left.

[EH]

71

Las Meninas

There are nine or eleven figures, including
dwarfs, handmaidens, and a reflection in
the dark, sharp-sighted mirror. And the artist
who hasn't yet begun the painting – which

is still patiently hidden from our eyes after
four centuries. Foucault posited the artist
was painting us. But, rather, perhaps model,
viewer and painter are all fragments of

a single prototype. There is more light than
could ever enter through the window (and,
as in paradise, its beneficence shines over

all imperfection). And there, where all the
gazes meet, is the incorporeal gaze, which
the paintbrush teaches us how to preserve.

[EH]

For R.K.

I only know that it is now over (or nearly) –
this black century, yet perhaps no blacker
than others. Still, it was different in scale.
It was consistent. Bodies became numbers,
souls ground to dross – into nothingness,
so that the mind might triumph. The abyss
touted as hope. I'd say, not without success.

Ovens loyally served the systems of pride.
In a nearby circle it was unyielding ice under
a stone star. The stifling carriages rolled on
towards nothing, westward and northward.
Nothing lasts. Empires' relics sink into dirt,
entwined with tough thistle and dock. While
megaphones fall mute, granite crumbling.

Born to this country, we prepare to depart –
but like Orpheus, we dare not turn around.
What accompanied us? Irony and patience,
very rarely, courage. Rather, a vague sense
you did much less than you should have.
(Is it a nagging guilt, or a sin, the children
won't forgive us – even if the Lord will?)

These were our choices. Yet we accepted
truth's bitter gift – we didn't extol death,
watched angels above rails and concrete,
fell in love, turned lights on in the library,
called good and evil by their names, seeing
how hard it is to tell them apart. This we
take into the dark. This is probably enough.

[EH]

Landscape, Summer 2001

(for Susan Sontag)

In the beginning was the wind, the signboards,
the tower breaking through the awkward gravel,
the wells of dingy courtyards, and the rounded
space of Parmenides extending upward.

The dust wafts to the groves in the outskirts.
An unseen butterfly clings to the volute,
and unremitting chance wipes out completely
a star's reflection in the quivering waters.

A loudspeaker by the open window
broadcasts the roar of the archangel's trumpet,
and God, upon waking, reduces
the square to a pinch of love and ashes.

The sun comes up above the ruined city.
Light gropes for the desk and quickly finds it,
and empty time is severed by a sentence
which contradicts the night that has just ended.

[CR]

Verses for a Child's Birth

Fate resembles only itself – fate.
Death only death. A child's experience
is different, and perhaps, simpler:
it ripens, like in the Book of Genesis.
In its cradle, as in Bethlehem's cave,
it senses light, and soon after, darkness.
It comes to know heaven's vault from the deep,
the continent's edge from the boundless sea
(so like its mother). Later it becomes
acquainted with grass, the sun and moon,
the rainbow of trout, armies of ravens
as they meander out across the sky.
With its awkward senses it seeks to tame
columns of chestnuts at the midday hour,
the world of buckthorn, snow, alder and cars,
the domesticated wolf, half-asleep,
and the wolf in the forest, which is but
nameless fear. Thus the Word draws near,
and our consciousness mixes with the Word,
repeating up above the 'let there be',
that suddenly suggests a strange meaning,
as we suspect that darkness – is ourselves,
while the light that exists is above us.

Henceforth, the child's affinity with the world
is stronger than to those who conceived it.
A secret thread connects it to mesons,
coal and diamonds – also the Amazon,
Mercury, the archangel, the cruel
Birnam Wood and the Ceryneian hind.

Some objects bend down to it, while others
rise in greeting. In a sound-filled wasteland,
between paradise lost and the trumpet,
it awakens, filled with the universe –
at once the hourglass and the sand, as
George Herbert once suggested. It often
believes that it is near the threshold
where all lines intersect, notes coincide
and where being attains its final goal.
Having read the Book of Genesis first,
we can only answer it with our deaths.

We are older and we already know,
that the notes wear away, the lines break off,
that air's expanses fail to capture sound
and inscriptions on paper fade away.
Only rarely, and by mistake, we meet –
in blind hope, in sympathy for matter,
in memory – which tries to take the place
of immortality, but can't always
succeed. Still for this, we should give thanks.
One cannot deny that it gives us strength,
when we descend to the valley, surrounded
by night, about which it's best to keep silent,
because we don't know yet if God hovers
above the empty, featureless waters.

[EH]

76

Pastoral

When into a canal's depth, choked
with duckweed, a bell's stroke falls
without echo: eyes closed, a stork
exercises its wings in unclear skies.
It listens to how the damp descends
from fern onto a violet's wick; how
the light, resembling night, glistens
on the landscape seen upside down.

A stain at the centre of the continent.
Beech and chestnut are in league here,
so you might not see the arrow's point
Actaeon aims at the spine of the boar.
The footpath, pale with dusty silver,
will not recognise the goddess's retinue.
A dragonfly will not disturb the hour.
The zodiac isn't born in the crepuscule.

The oars fall silent. The heart lets off –
while the clouds that flood the ford,
divide like the nature of being itself:
made up of non-being and the Word.

[EH]

FROM

Winter Dialogue

(1997)

Translations by
DIANA SENECHAL

A Poem About Memory

You wait for the departed? Into the depths
They have departed. The walls abandoned them,
As did the pictures, pencils, clocks and souls,
The rain and retribution, sand and snow,
The pine needles, the victory over death.

Already there's no telling who is right,
And when you add up all the partings,
Your aimless sum explodes inside,
And shatters into voices, fiercely warring.

These things remain: a circle drawn by a knife,
Dust on the shelves, a mark on a plate,
Such wealth of freedom, verses and untruth,
And such a shortage of authentic fate.

Two voices also stay. They touch the warm,
Uncomfortable volume of this city.
To them a drop of memory was given.
It is yours. And it belongs to none.

It runs at random, winged, blind from birth,
Like a swallow cast out from its nest.
And what is all your classicism worth,
That school of ceremony and of jest?

And thus the hour, detaching from us all,
Condemned to death, flutters down like a shawl
Onto the stairways, corridors and rooms,
And on the gap, which, disregarding, sprawls
Between the time gone by and time to come.

Winter Dialogue

Enter this landscape. Darkness still prevails.
Filled to the brim with voices, though unseen,
The continent takes up arms against the seas.
Across the dunes, the empty highway wails.
A passerby or an angel in the snow
Has left a subtle covered trail behind,
And, in the blackish pane, the seaside's glow
Becomes the bleak Antarctic in our minds.

The chasm, not frozen, froths beneath the land.
The pouring grains of sand pass their first mile.
Sometimes the pier grows vivid, sometimes veiled,
And, menacingly, the winter space expands.
No telegrams, no letters stay behind,
Just photographs. No sound from the transistor.
A candle, you would say, has sealed the time
Of danger with its burning hot wax drippings.

How sonorous the rock, how damp the air,
How mighty the radiation when it forestalls
The dawn! You strain your eyes until the walls,
Church tower, human body turn transparent.
Only the hazy contours of the trees
Stand out against the whiteness. Through the bark,
Even closing your eyes, you almost see
The stubborn, narrow last ring of the trunk.

'This habit has been trying on my eyes;
In just a minute, I will surely falter.'
'The prophecy is speaking of another.'
The hoarfrost-covered axis now inclines,
And, at the line of the horizon, where
The ships turn black, where the vibration freezes,
A flame bursts forth from Mars and Jupiter,
Deep in the sluggish sky, above the seaside.

The void extends to the Atlantic sand.
The field gapes like a hall, open and barren.
While January blankets February,
The plain shrinks back from the watery wind.
Past the lagoons, the hills begin to bare
Themselves; a somewhat melted snowdrift stiffens
And darkens in a pit. 'And what is there?'
'Again the ports and bays, the mouths of rivers.'

Beneath the screen mesh of the weighty cloud,
Squares, like fish, are glittering and playing.
'Do you remember what the stars were saying?'
'This century is managing without
A sign; there's just statistics.' 'Gravity
Of death has fettered person, plant, and thing,
But sprouts burst forth from seed and sacrifice,
And then not all is over, or so I think.'

'Where is the witness? Still it's not too clear
What separates the real from the imagined;
Perhaps just you and I are on this planet.'
'It seems to me that only you are here.'
'And what about the third one? Do you mean
That no one hears us talking, or takes part?'
'There is the firmament and snowy green,
And the voice, at times, lives longer than the heart.'

The stroke of noon brings dark hues to the woods.
When day attains its height, consciousness
Retains light things, brought forth from nothingness
A moment ago, taking the place of words:
A piece of ice, split into particles,
A skeleton of boughs, a brick wall, crumbled
Beside the roadway's bend... Then all is silence
On this side of the sea, and on the other.

*　*　*

I was welcomed by twilight and cold.
Past the stark and ponderous arches
Some ten stations began to unfold,
And umpteen November parks:
This circle, or settled place,
Where the beam of a hundred-watt bulb,
Angling into the maze,
Deceptively hits the brick wall.

The realm of Ariadne and Minos
Becomes a new home, though soon ended;
Because of the fog, not one plane
In the past few hours has ascended.
How packed the trains are, every day –
So much space, so much air and hardship!
Thus the prisoners, wending their way
Homeward, sometimes ached for the guard.

Like a debt that space was repaying,
The places I knew resurfaced.
'University, bus,' I was saying,
'Island, monument,' over and over.
I said: 'Tomorrow I'm leaving,
Or at least I will try to depart.'
And there, at the edge of the living,
My soul plunged into the dark.

Old street names and numbers came close,
Form and meaning had changed in each letter.
I followed the vanishing voices,
Unable to find us together
In the apartment, bolted and empty,
Where the pictures don't know me, nor even
In dreams, or the kingdom of heaven,
Or the second circle of Dante.

Thus time is cut short: to be clear,
One does not lose the habit of living,
Only, I would say, with each year,
From farther you hear the phone ringing.
Only memory, as the days pass,
Widens itself like a compass,
Until a straight line is the past
That once made a pretence at distance.

In reality cut from reality,
What you hear or perceive, I don't know.
The paved banks of the Acheron
Withstood the insensible flow.
Each nothingness stands on its own,
And without us the world still persists,
And the Muses and silence alone
Can, in truth, be said to exist.

Where the capital spins in a ring,
And the snow games make us weary,
Where fog won't betray the things,
Thank God for the dictionary.
In the land where the hand of a friend
Never rushes to help one in anguish,
The highest power, or the void
Sends the angel down: rhythm and language.

I don't ask for a minute's oblivion,
Or death, or sins' forgiveness,
But leave the primordial moan
Over icy night and stone.

To the Memory of a Poet. Variation

In Petersburg we will come together anew.
OSIP MANDELSTAM

Did you return to the once promised place,
The city's skeleton, reflection, trace?
A blizzard swept the Admiralty away,
The geometric hue fades into gloom
Upon the surface.
                           Turning off the electric
Current, a shadow rises from the spectrum
Of ice, and rusty steam engines, like spectres,
Near Izmailov Prospect rise and loom.

The same tram, the very same threadbare coat...
The asphalt makes a shred of paper float
Above it, and the nineteenth-century cold
Submerges train and station.
                           Wailing skies
Enclose themselves. The decades turn to mist,
The murky cities pass, like storms adrift,
The gestures are repeated, like a gift,
But from the dead a man does not arise.

He retreats into a February morning,
Which has encompassed Rome, sluggish and northern,
Into another space, choosing a rhythm
Approximated to the hour of snow.
He's summoned to the she-wolf's lair, now frozen,
The mental institution, filth and prison,
The black, familiar Petersburg, arisen
In someone or other's speech some time ago.

Not harmony, nor measure, once they're quelled,
Return to life, nor the crackling, nor the smell
Inside the hearth, which time has kindled well;
Yet there exists a timeless hearthlike focus
And optics, mapping destiny, whose essence
Consists of fortunate coincidences,
Or simply meetings and continuations
Of what is neither temporal nor local.

No image, but a breach in what is known,
An island, grown into the current's foam,
The substitute for paradise not found
Arise in living language. In the shower
Of clouds, above the stem of a ship afloat,
The pigeons move in a giant circle, not
Presuming to distinguish Ararat
From any ordinary hill in flower.

Forsake this shore. It's time. We will embark.
The lie runs dry, the stones are split apart,
But there remains a single witness: art,
Bringing light into the nights of winter's depth.
The blessed grasses overcome the ice,
The mouths of rivers find the bays at night,
And a word, as meaningless as it is light,
Resounds, almost as meaningless as death.

Nel Mezzo Del Cammin Di Nostra Vita

(to the memory of Konstantin Bogatyrev)

Midcentury has overtaken me.
I lived, but learned not to exist at that.
Death came along and joined the family,
Claiming the greater portion of my flat.
I'd try to tame her, little by little,
Imploring her not to extend her hand,
And, in the mornings, I'd observe the city,
The loveliest of Eastern Europe's land,
As far as I know: where iron awaits its stroke,
Where rotting rushes rustle in the mist,
There's a locomotive, knuckle-duster, rock,
Perhaps a bit of gasoline at best.
Within this death, I'd sleep, I'd drink, I'd eat,
I'd try to give her a meaning and a goal,
I'd even let her slip my mind. But meet
Her casually – that's almost impossible.

I'd turn the key in the corridor. The breath
Would lose its rhythm; the heart would drop its weight
Onto the chest. To tell the truth, death
Could even be fortuitous in this state.

The Shield of Achilles

(to Joseph Brodsky)

I speak only to see upon the screen
Of nerves, as you once saw, in vivid tones,
The fences near the chapels of stone,
The key beside the ashtray dumped clean.
You weren't wrong: it's all the same as here.
Even the volume of imagination.
The same kilometres toward the ocean,
      Which lends an ear

To us at night. Under the roof of leaves,
The heavy lamps are similar in their shining.
The different tempos in the chimings
Suggest more danger than the bitter wave
Dividing us. Withdrawing into space,
You become an unknown, like the Medes
And Greeks. We remained on this ship to meet
      Only disgrace –

Since it's not safe, not even for a rat.
Examine it: it's not a ship at all,
But shining roofs, calamities, brick walls,
The date recurring all too fast –
In a word, the age of maturity. Its wardship
Seeps through to the marrow, and its space,
Making more waste each day, would blur the gaze,
      If, by the border

(The ruminating ground for upright rain),
The solemn arch of sound were not to arise,
Almost destroyed in this summer of surprise,
But instead presenting us with blessed chains
Which coincide, probably, with the soul –
They stigmatise, determine, raise the form,
Because our skies, because our *terra firma*
        Are the voice alone.

Peace be with you. Peace be with me and you.
Let there be darkness. Let the seconds tumble.
Through dense vastness, through layers of slumber,
I split your words apart and read them through.
The cities disappear. In nature's stead
There's just a white shield, which has outweighed
Non-being. Both our eras will be played
        Out on its face

(If only force and time were not so stingy!)
As in the water. Or, to be exact,
As in the emptiness. The billows thrash,
Wiping away the living scene. The windows
Glisten in squares of blackness. In a dream,
The heated air sifts through the glass slowly.
Far in the distance, past the towers, screams
        A motor, rolling

The hours onto me. At times one can see
In the dark: you see a bell swaying,
You see an endless interval fraying,
While the foundation answers silently.
The stricken portals shudder, tightening,
The arch sends out a signal to its neighbour,
And souls and continents invoke each other
       In the breathing night.

The dirty fog sticks to the sails at dock.
The wet embankment warms and clouds with steam.
You see Thermopylae, and Troy you've seen –
You have received a shield. You are a rock.
Pillars, erected on that fortitude,
Plunge sparkling metal into the wind,
Although not far from stillness does it stand,
       Or from untruth.

Entrusting us with all our destinies,
You enter the plateau of recollections.
But every moment, doubled into fractions,
And twinning light becomes our company
Inside a circle, narrowing more and more.
Low tide. The sand is patched with gleaming puddles.
The eye still can't distinguish stone from rudder
       On the empty shore.

The Eleventh Canto

How is this, Elpenor, how could you journey to the western gloom
swifter afoot than I in the black lugger?

ODYSSEY 11.57-58

I suppose this never happened. Through the branches
We saw a large and desolated harbor.
The concrete pier was bleaching peacefully
In shade, on the water encumbered with silt.
The splintered piles protruded from the breakers.
The wind, once barely leaping above the plain,
Now teased the sandy whirlpool, darker than
The smashed ribs of the vessels. The savage air,
Transfixed by masts, entwined in ropes, lay heavy
On the thistle, the dunes, the stretch of water.
On the horizon, the heat was fluttering,
As a tattered flag might. A fellow who
Had hammered up a raft of rotten planks
Took it for a ride down the stream. It seemed
He would have been heartened by some companions.
Besides him, we saw no one on the shore.
Someone had told us once that this site,
Like many sites, resembled Ithaca.

We stood there, in the focus of the day.
The war of bygone ages and the voyage
Were filling our brains, just as a wave
Fills up the bronchus of a reckless swimmer.
Crunching beneath our feet: the mussels, bones,
And porous pebbles. Then we lay down on
The grass, with nature off our minds. And nature
Had cleared us from her mind long before.

The firmament flowed by. The rumbling salt,
Incited by the shrouded moon, rehashed
Its cycle. Floats were soaking in the sea.
On the logs, bound together by iron,
Beneath the sun's full blaze, the molluscs glittered.

What murkiness, what patient depth arrives
With every breaker! How the foam resounds –
Now in memory's hole, now close at hand,
Between the dredger's backbone and the pier.

A rustle passed us by and disappeared:
A traveller, bearing an oar on his shoulder,
Headed for the land, where no one ever
Had seen an oar. And, at the foot of the dune,
A field mouse, darting, shot a sudden eye
At the trident rusting on the sand.

There is no wave. Rather, there is a force,
But not the sum of drops. Within each second,
The water parts with itself. Equator of death,
Cramped island, grass beneath the palm of the hand,
Return, change. Not even this
Is promised us by history and myth.

Beyond the bend, a change crept over the scene.
At first the perspectives moved slightly.
Each grain of sand, gleaming along the way,
Came to our eyes through a magnifying glass,
And rocks appeared through reversed binoculars.
The outlines of the objects blurred, as would
Sounds in a shapeless hall. Soon all of us
Concluded that the heat must be the cause,
And suffered no surprise, when, by the warehouse,
We met a friend – the very first of those
To be encountered only after death.

He was the first.

*　　*　　*

We've been seized by the pull of the universe since September began.
Shut your eyes, and you'll sense how a leaf, having brushed past your face,
Flutters into a shutter, and brushes a cloud by mistake,
And gets stuck in a tile, so as not to be reached by the hand.

The tree drains the day. The heavens are blinded and white.
Wading into the waterfall valley, the voice is receding.
I have been singled out to grasp how the stillness inside
And the steam of the bath brought gladness to wearied Atrides.

Will you conquer this threshold? Destiny, castle, crushed stone,
Wretched churches of flint, muddy triangular spaces,
Into putrid decay, into sand the expansive hour pours,
The metropolis soars, and the twelve winds swoop upward to chase it.

Will you win me or lose – for now, there's no way to discern.
These soils are shallow, the constellar thicket is felled.
I attract misfortune, just as the north pulls a magnet,
As magnet pulls magnet, misfortune attracts me in turn.

*   *   *

Glimmer a smile, stand still, then take the path back home –
Outside, the darkness tries to rob the eyes of sight,
But still the syllable, reviving on my tongue,
Will bless and supersede this year's most endless night.
Glimmer a smile, since we are separated by
The plain, icy lakes, blizzards, allowing no translucence,
The curtain, which you see as sleep invades your brain,
And murky trains running from Daugavpils to Luga.

The kitchen has a cool spring, drying at the mouth,
And several chairs scattered around like a meagre forest.
I also fall asleep, and the meaning of this house
Is just a mailing address, a disc with finger-holes.
I also fall asleep; it seems that from the table
I pick up the receiver. It's ruinous to linger,
Since, left with you alone, on waking I am able
To hear myself on the other end when I stop my finger.

*   *   *

All night, sleep was equivalent to time,
And the city shot needles into my face.
I don't know what's in store. Perhaps the currents –
They flash beneath the windows, all the way,
Reflecting the staunchness of the mountain chain.
Snow from the skies, piling heavy on streetlamps,
The arcadia of grasses, empty squares.
Better to forget. All is untruth, after all,
Only passageways sunken into frost.
Here, with your hands you sense the stellar vault,
Porous like stones. Here, you would have to live
For centuries – and swim along with the flow
Around each date as if it were an island.
Space filled with dots of light, a heavy crystal
Between the fingers of the Caucasus.
Better to forget. All is untruth, after all.
Experiences, approximations, beginnings.
I can no longer say what touches us:
Perhaps just air, sprouting beneath the snow,
Having taken this night to learn by heart
Our lofty science, rife with imperfections.

*   *   *

Shoots of grass pierce one's face and hands.
Glory to poverty. The earth is made of roses.
The resistance of matter, the soil of Voronezh
Are like the past and like forgotten friends.

Some umpteen planets lie beneath the heart,
And Dante's circles press against the windows,
So close at hand is the path that seeks me out,
Itself now shaken by an ominous ringing.

Joined sentences will scorch the fingertips:
Embittered bread, the weary brain, the fallow
Meadows, whose care is plunged into the valley,
The clan of airy capitals of the sphere...

* * *

To the squares on our walls and floors,
And squares upon the doors,
To the high windowpanes – twice more,
And to the lamp – twice more,
To names of amputated shores,
To gates of maps, and to
The air not being jumbled, or
The inside jumbled too.
To locomotive wheels that roar,
Keys tested long before,
To all of us, those two times four,
Those times that number four.
To that which from the wires will pour,
Which ice cannot ignore,
To two and two still making four,
And two times two – still four.

*   *   *

Desist, desist. The crumbling sentence dies.
The rooftops' limit verges on the dawn.
The snow speaks forth, the fire in fugue replies.

The swinging of the pendulum subsides;
The leaden counterbalance marks the ground.
Desist, desist. The crumbling sentence dies.

Reflected in the mirror's wasteland eyes,
Instead of the world, an outline gleams alone.
The snow speaks forth, the fire in fugue replies.

And back into the cell the captive strides,
And skyward wades the fencing of the zone.
Desist, desist. The crumbling sentence dies.

A grain of time, a splinter of the skies
Envelops both our bodies, like a globe.
The snow speaks forth, the fire in fugue replies.

Things cling to the face only to vaporise,
And bedposts have no angels around.
Desist, desist. The crumbling sentence dies.
The snow speaks forth, the fire in fugue replies.

An Attempt at Describing a Room

o the pillows and the palettes and the earrings made of gold
but the map will never show it as the address is annulled

but the boulevard is glowing and the tea turns into air
but the wires stretch into nowhere and the essence is unclear

tongue of flame begins to flicker midnight strikes you as you write
and the lobsters shrimp and fish break through the canvas with their sight

since the border of the fishbowl stretches out our windowpane
where the blind and artless shepherds tend the nutshells in the brine

hardness sets the liquid plaster you i cease to hear or see
void of gratitude and happy underneath the spreading tree

Sestina

It's roughly six o'clock, and the ice-covered road
Swerves to the north. Strapped to the tyres, the chains
Rattle the road. A voiceless steel echo,
Like the lake's surface, glimmers a reflection.
The weightless wound-inflicted March snow
Still tries to cover the demolished forest.

Like a raft, splitting apart the static forest,
The glance halts. It is deluded by the road,
The severalfold self-duplicating snow,
And birches making monotonic chains.
In the mist, the well's lever rises, reflecting
The empty house. And all the rest is echo

And clots of air. An aimless, homeless echo,
Which does not exist, sends rumbles through the forest.
The graphite mirror blackens, reflecting
The vaulting dark. We have been given a road
And sky-born, sky-matured, sky-banished chains:
Invisible, but all-consuming snow.

Spring's old age falls beneath the watch of snow,
And hearing is torn by the many-faced echo.
Like a dam, wresting its way out of its chains,
A blind thought soaks itself into the forest.
Here gasoline won't help, nor the white road,
Nor the strip of clearing, unfolding its reflection.

The formless universe pours its reflection.
A shiver-giving star, the reason-stealing snow
Besiege the plain and arm themselves for the road.
Reflection, shadow, reproduction, echo
Refill the overtumbled Arden forest;
Their changes constitute the only chains.

Will we be ever tempered by Thy chains?
All things and elements rise, reflecting
Myself. I will forsake this murky forest,
Where trees are cloaked and guarded by the snow,
And words give over to a futile echo,
And all comes to an end. Perhaps the road

Itself is chains. I am denied the road
Into Thy forest. The earth is numbed by snow.
We're enemies reflecting. Thou art an echo.

Ode to a City

Although I won't be able
To shake you, still I will,
I'll put out every taper:
The tower and the bell,
The stony streets, the shore
Bedecked with tar, and even
My soul, though I'm not sure
It counts among the living.

Here, underneath my feet,
The shaky roadway crumbles.
The shooting range, unlit,
Conceals a dark-voiced rumble
Of waves, a vast expanse,
And, from the days of Noah,
Above the depths, the dance
Of Aquilon and Notus.

Fires of loneliness sail
Above the salt abyss,
Above death's crystal hall.
There, empty trolleys stream
Around the theatre's corner,
The crowds of bridges swim,
And a lifeless pine-filled forest
Takes footsteps in a dream.

I cannot see Orion,
But the spume emits a glow.
The clouds, in double row,
Let the horizon through.
The wet tree seems a nerve
Beside the wretched granite,
And Aquilon and Eurus
Rotate the sky around it.

Will you disappear or wallow
In my eyelids' darker side?
Having closed my eyes, I follow
The final splash of light.
Eternity will flood us,
But under my hand these stall:
The patience of your gardens,
The weight of your stone walls.

No fortresses, no laurels
Adorn the trampled wild,
The grasses that poked holes in
The tense magnetic field,
The void, dripping, decaying,
Soaking the head in chill,
And frenzied Boreas flaying
Beyond the nameless hill.

The clear gust of the ether
Finds echoes in the grasses.
Will you rule or will you wither
In memory's recesses?
It seems that ruin prevails –
And, guilty to the brim,
My greedy mouth assails
Your remaining oxygen.

Time inundates the road.
The cliffs approach in haste.
May Aeolus, if God
Is absent, keep you safe.

Two Poems About Love

I

When, in private, unstable wisdom is sent from a height,
And fragments of stairway chatter come rolling down,
Above the muddy garden, befriended by night,
Above the wasteland, flutes and harps are born.

Beneath the sandy slope, the dry riverbed
Comes to life, the round drop pierces the steaming stone,
The orchestra's rumble rises, the end is ahead,
Which, as you know, requires neither word nor form.

Salt on the mouth. Brine bespeckles the brow.
The city sprawls like a whale cast onto the sand.
A twisted fragment of space, by which the reckless
White flight of converging souls will come to an end.

An angular star gleams in the slit of the eyes,
The impulsive universe provides a galactic lens,
And your life – a swallow surmounting the earth – alights,
Burdens the shoulder, flutters, and makes no sound.

It's not worth looking around; we're long surrounded,
Confined in the muddle of aerial waterfalls,
Invisible landslides, grey clouds, melody bounding –
It fills our mouths and sticks to the alveoli.

And all returns. I remember those verses by heart.
Having tilted, the sleepless houses turn to the left.
Under ridges of roofs, the darkness is spread apart,
And wearied hands turn the sky like a sail adrift.

II

The streets lose their names, I expect no more guests,
The iamb of others is absent at best,
And even, it seems, the heavens, forbidden,
Have abandoned my thoughts. But space has remained,
For the glittering water floods in, all the same,
And carries the overturned tower along with it.

Three dimensions squeak, like linked chain mail.
Reflection plays with them; when the skies pale,
It fades, and the empty abode receives
Maybe darkness of May, maybe darkness of June,
And a lifetime is short, and that is untrue,
Since the lamp, in the meantime, protects us from evil.

Don't rush, it's not time. The children still sleep,
The miracle waits to be born. Pools and creeks
Grow cold, roofs blacken, and summertime ripens,
And voices and landscapes in separate dreams
Pass each other like boats. When day comes along,
We'll endeavour to misunderstand them, most likely.

The sonorous–dark, cloven thicket of forms
Oppresses our consciousness; it's not known
Whether even one line coincides, or a fraction,
But our bodies, like stones, still lie side by side,
And the fortress grows clear in the quadrate of light,
And Cassandra's epiphanies lose their attraction.

*   *   *

Write a poem about a conversation with birds.
FROM A LETTER

Although the well is bottomless and steep,
The oriole, reed, human, constellation
Dare to peer into the brilliant deep –
United by an unforseen relation.

It often seems that this is all the same
One light refracted through a sounding prism.
Your truth and dust, what difference can they claim
From all the thrush's silvery sophisms?

Before the dawn, when summer ends its course,
When vaults scatter and worlds fall to the ground,
One and the same unconscious, sightless force
Strikes you, a frail lyre, into sudden sound.

*   *   *

In the indigent cities, it's time to leave friends behind us.
The floating lamps shed their barren light in blessing.
The night loses us; the bumpy pine forests, resin
And needly sky of the road to Aukštadvaris find us.

Yes, this is Thy space that suddenly grows and thickens.
Thou drawest us close to the finish line, then far.
Thou contractest my pupil, after stretching the field of vision
To the shadow of the hand, to the blind tarpaulin.

And if my generation is not destined to win the race,
May the first one not feel the need, in his short life to follow,
Of his daily bread and not-so-everyday fate,
Of his daily salt and not-so-everyday water.

May they find me at last: his perfect voice, broken away,
The atonement for untruth, the beginning of trouble and freedom –
Thus the Nemunas water is bound to be black and sweetish,
That the waning moon, turning to vapor, may float to the bay.

Ghetto

We'll certainly return here. This is peace.
So many homes. With the uncanny ease
Of coal, all has been numbered, weighed, divided.
This is the final hour.
                              Betrayal tightens
And seals the glass displaying random bits
Of news, flows through the doorway's yellow chink,
Colours the armband, condemns the bond and ink
To death, and loads a burden on the nets.

Ah, childlike thoughts, a house on shaky grounds,
Abated waters, artificial mounds!

There is no death, and judgement will not come.
The window's frame is licked by sand and flame.
No more by laws of ancient Hebrew times,
Or Roman – by the one and final law
We are no more than letters, footnotes, dashes.
We are untainted paper. We are ashes.

A Poem About Friends
(for Natalia Gorbanevskaia)

When even strangers lose the mark of strangeness,
And all those things that had no chance to pass
Leave downward with the flow of non-existence –
Assuming non-existence has a path –
When, past the city, day comes to a close,
And, following a storm, the radio rumbles,
We won't be able to turn or lock ourselves
Outside of the last minutes of this summer.

The air grows dark; through the doors enter
The exiled, the detained, the disappeared,
For whom, this very night, our room turns into
The only possible Elysian field,
The ones whose shadows wander in our dreams,
Those who have loved each other and forgotten,
Make the depths of mirrors their uncertain home,
And, without warning, rise up from the bottom.

Thus they are raised from the dead underground:
The winged women and the unseen brothers,
The generation long reduced to sound,
To margins, or to grass thirsting for water,
And those who live are chosen by the fog,
Deserted houses, journeys into the distance,
Their weapons are staunchness, abstinence from speech,
And possibly, Apollo's own assistance.

The rooftop will resemble Nature's edge,
The night will disentangle thaw from frost,
And, even with death nearby, the spoken word
Will nonetheless be worthy of our trust,
If, poisoning all thought and all sensation,
And hollowing a hole in stone stairs,
An uninvited future should await them:
The object they gave up and then made theirs.

They frequented our forests. Like the pines,
Dead furniture preserves the finger smudges.
Now, having met the maturity of time,
They no longer depend on earthly judges.
It is an open, ample family,
Whose children have been given just one name –
And emptiness, forcing the voices free,
Refills our vacuum up to the very brim.

I do not believe in calamity, but rather
In friends, to whom I gave in equal shares
The distance separating eyes from matter:
Infinity, unnatural and scarce.
All faces disappear into the light,
The lamps flicker out, truths are divulged,
But footsteps reach a meeting-point inside
Myself, just as parallel lines converge.

And again it's autumn, full of lavish folly.
Inside the city, which some souls have won,
Above the alien trolleycars and dwellings,
At this very hour, September has begun.
Imposing barges stand affixed to piers,
Since morning, every nerve is wound up tight,
And, on the road, the first leaf that appears
Is crooked, like the armour of a knight.

Thanksgiving Day

At the foot of the slope, the marsh stinks of metal.
A horse nibbles the urchin-like grass.
Eight women toil at tables at the center
Of autumn and the plain. Dew saturates
The Ohio weekend. Down in the ravine,
A maple tree is rusting (or a tin can,
No way to tell). Lights thickening their beams,
Wisconsin, the Dakotas, Oregon,

Orion too. The landslide of the Lord
Onto the lost space. While the monotone
Of heartbeats smashes the severe ground,
Let thanks be given for the new land.
I can't grasp it, but it is alive.
It can't grasp me, yet I would assume
That the aged dog would sooner recognise
Odysseus here than in his native home.

I offer my thanksgiving for the answers
The sleepless mind is weary of pursuing.
For the new water. For grasses belonging
To the future. For the patient wind
Over them. For the future foreign grave,
For the benign weight of the stone upon it,
For non-existence. And for Thee, Who can
Draw something from it. If Thou dost will it.

For the black music of the spheres. And for
The containment of it in this day's rotation.
Accustomed to the twilight, objects are
Repeated on this side of the ocean.
Corners fill, as three clocks arise.
The retina, not afraid of a mistake,
Discovers a lock, a tablecloth, the stars
Just as in childhood, in the same old place.

Autumn in Copenhagen

From the mouth of a dragon
the Baltic waters come pouring. A bronze claw flashes,
the sharp-edged current, curling up whiplike, lashes
itself into steam
at the fountain's mouth.
No instant cure can be found for memory's breaches,
and, above Copenhagen, the familiar rain cloud approaches
from the left,

if you look to the south.
It is joined by tin roofs, by branchless mud-covered lindens,
by bicycles, thousands of bicycles. Hastily hidden
in the water, an echo has leaped
to the surface, beside the port's gates.
The asters are damp. The attics parade their geraniums loudly,
the vertical line of the barge entraps the sidewalk, resounding
in the channel, whose depths

are opaque. You might say
only statues can conquer this autumn. The wet king extends
his hand to the bishop. The letters, the crosses engraved on the stands
are nibbled away
by the void of brine,
since history ends. The countries and states disappear.
Having lent your ear, you can hear: from the pole October draws near,
and winter behind.

The dim neon pounds
on the boulevard's corner. A traveller sets down his bags,
looks at Anna's square, touches branches, silently asks
what city he's found,
since the day
overflows with the black taste of home. A sailboat bumps
the shore, and the name from the north, the crowded consonant lump
in the mouth, rolls smoothly away.

The solid stucco is laden
with crucified bindweeds, with leaf-stars and roses,
a resonant railway past Tivoli opens and closes,
the incoming train
is never delayed.
Not that thing called beauty lies under the pupils, but sand
mixed with lime, a cheek's contour, the touch of a hand,
the horizon's line.

You're compelled
to let your shoulders fall back on the thickening wind,
to scoop up the salt and silt you know, but within
the inscrutable well
the level falls every second,
and so many times you have offered thanksgiving and paid
for your exile in cash, having chosen your personal fate.
You won't answer the beckon

of home, since each atom stationed
in your body has long been replaced. Dislodged
consciousness fumbles
through language, as if through a drawer. Moods, adjectives humming,
negations,
the blindness
of infinite particles, crowded sentences, and, only now and then,
the dry, as if unfamiliar, but breath-stopping pain
and silence.

A cloudburst of rays
sets a crown on the spiral tower. You pass a brick wall
as if you blew out a candle. Baroque architecture must fall
as dictated by space,
and, instead of the bricks,
beyond the bushes and wasteland, sand meets the debris
of *mare*, *pelagos*, *thalassa*, sea, the singular sea,
as wide as the Styx.

And over the brinks
of crests, and over breaches of foam,
lead converges in piles, predicting oblivion and storm.
The flat mainland stinks
of squalid ore,
and the radio misfires. There remains of the homeland, all told,
just a soundless threat, a leaking uranium whale
on the crags of the shore.

For now, you exist.
Granite directs the stage; with the willows' cues
in the face of noon, the park sheds its yellow leaves,
the barometer clenches its fist
at the shimmering depth.
Cold pierces through to the bones. No salvation from sweater
or jacket,
and Telemark ice is the wind, and fog is the breath of Kattegat,
and death is death.

All told, this prevails: apprehending the sound of a punctual train,
caressing the face of a stranger, hands on the rails,
when, in error, the whole dictionary
coincides with the pronoun 'we'.
The magnesium frost gives a glow to the tray, the sheets,
and the traveller clenches his teeth, numbly shooting his seed
to the depths of a wearied womb.

Never again
to go home. To wrap yourself up, and vanish
in the fortress of fall, relinquish what you must relinquish,
and this still ahead,
a trace of the previous land.
And hearts are still beating, however sinful and shameful that might
appear, and the siren's pure wail interferes with the sullied night
on this side of the Sound.

Sheremetyevo, 1977

Having passed through the cold of customs, the line of armed guards,
Having climbed the stairs to a meagre heaven of currency,
I suddenly realised that I hadn't waved to a few who remained behind.

Even before the plane took off, they were forever transformed into shadows,
Echoes in the pit of the telephone, addresses in a half-forgotten little book,
And that is the only miracle of our time.

I knew that the voices would crumble and the words would turn into dust,
A familiar face would withdraw into the twilight of photographs,
When bookshelves and lamps finally crowded it out.

I didn't know who was Persephone's captive: I or they.
From the little table I looked at the flat expanse through the glass:
The body I abandoned, as a poet from these parts once said.

There, next to the electric power station, the soaked sun will sag soon,
The tram cars will rustle, splashing mud on the March boulevards,
The ponds will thaw by Grand Georgian Street.

There, at some other time, near the many-windowed postwar wall,
A suicide lay face downward, the militia drove the people away,
And I didn't grasp at once what that signified.

Since that moment, I've been given enough time to understand:
Twelve, twenty, or even thirty years
In dark rooms, on vast and dark continents.

And, in the same place almost, a key squeaked in response to a knock,
And, in the same place almost, I learned how a line shines,
Illuminating the midnight trees and snow.

A country not one's own, entrusted like a temporary body,
The marshy land of the unvictorious, up to the Barents Sea,
The crosses of airplanes above the invisible sky.

*   *   *

Bit by bit, at the edge of the unforeseen land,
Dreams change in the sultry weather,
And language will likely give way after them,
Since it also will not last forever.

In speech, no blackness of pines will be left,
No ravine of rough-faced fall,
Nor the wet and golden terrain of death,
Where a glacier knocks on the wall.

They retreat: the denouement, the swampy voices,
And, replete with untruth, the vastness,
And, disclaiming the voice, you listen close
To another body's distant darkness.

All night you listen to another's blood flow,
Where you live, as if in a mirror,
Where the heavy reflection leaves no glow
In the Neva or in the Neris.

*   *   *

I have learned to see in the dark, to distinguish happiness from happiness,
to understand what the closeness of another's life can mean,
to grasp unexpectedly the changes in the time of year,
the way two or three atoms add weight to the air at noon.
A reflection in the window, vanished half a moment ago,
a voice mixed into the leaves, breathing's scrambled traces
were repeating to me that you had returned to town before
a friend, a well-wisher, an enemy, God Himself was able
to say it. Like a Delphic fugitive, you hid
in the boles of cherry trees, elms, you changed, shifted the calendar,
having turned away from the ray, having turned almost into untruth
and non-existence – that which is unable to grant
even a drop of itself. Here the exchange is always uneven;
Phoebus is alive thanks to you, while you exist on your own
(what myth guesses, what Verbum and Logos have hidden,
we will grasp with ease, I think, when we cross the finish line)

and now, when the reflectors' echo thunders a double start,
when concrete and wheels fly apart by a millimetre,
like a blizzard to one in Siberia, a name burns the throat,
a name that literally means snowy weather.
The wet curved mainland mirrors your features.
It's unclear whether stars are circling, or a wind is plunging,
and there's not much reality. The play of wind and waters,
the universe of clouds over Geneva, Varna, London.
Werther is already forgotten. All the places in the world
are marked in a diary. The word 'I love' is erased.
A crash is much closer, even the homeland and the Lord
are closer than the body and soul just fifteen miles from this place.

There are no more signs in the sky, but still one can see and hear
in the final darkness, before the era of ice or fire.
It has been said that there will be no more time. Two thousand years,
two drops, two airplanes roll through the hemisphere.

A Museum in Hobart

The country has been desolate for ages.
The pendulum of waves, the basalt's din.
I'll be more precise. A segment of the natives,
having survived three assaults on their kin,
signified nothing. Here's the cape, where later
they all turned into dust. A nomad folk,

naked and hungry. At the very edge,
which a poet sees involuntarily;
without a past. And almost without speech.
Before last year, there was a skeleton here,
but they burned it – perhaps to show respect,
or take over the space it had claimed for years.

The place can't tolerate a void. I hear
space turn, I hear the breaches close.
A new beginning overcomes this sphere
at the hands of several artists, tempters, rogues,
usually not too guilty. To be clear,
a British Gulag, modest in its scope,

which, later, in the deluge of non-being,
went under. Here is the globe's most peaceful place.
What happened, happened. 'No' was spoken. Even
the tape recorder repents these mistakes,
and the autochthon menaces on the screen
good-naturedly, having returned from space

eternal: the low brow, inclining pate,
unwounded by the bloodstained clawlike thorns.
Today the powers' wardship would elate
even the dead. There language, you would own,
would be enriched as well – although, for that,
what's there to talk about within these zones?

Perhaps about how, on the line of time,
the prisons and the world are getting better.
A casino. Down by the stone circle,
your bronchi catch the wind, the sails glitter,
and he who finds the city a cosy home
does not return the ticket to the Creator,

nor to the Ansett Company. A hush.
A tribe without a feature or a trace.
Chains under the resistant glass. A grosz-
like history, worn underfoot, erased,
and, from the wreath of bay and ridge, the gush
of Antarctic mists, like ancient sea-spun lace.

This axe beside the roots. This rock. We are
no longer brothers, but neighbours anyway,
where time meets time like a perpendicular,
where our photographs and alphabets decay,
the splintered syllable, the ash and tar
still cry out something from the tourist display.

What is oblivion? Where is oblivion going?
Clepsidras trickle, baby rivers flow.
Along the crowded universe or nothing,
the lampshade sways, despair bursts into glow
at times. Sandstone slabs, a pier, the night,
signs on the wind. Drawings on the snow.

* * *

How late the cafés open,
And how fresh is the print of the damp newspaper!

BORIS PASTERNAK

Before the middle of July, Paris
Is empty. Not a single phone replies,
Or else it answers in a borrowed voice,
Announcing that the number has changed somewhat
Since last year. The eloquent recording
Does not wish to reveal the latest cipher.
Why, you can't be so unaware by now,
We'll say, these things are no longer a secret:
Around the bend, the ruined Place des Vosges,
A winged courtyard genius, a balcony,
Unstable arches, propped up with logs, just as
In Užupis. A sleepy labourer
Chisels the roadway. In the sultry air,
A swallow draws the outline of a face
Preserved in memory just about as much
As any face. A motor has a coughing fit,
And then you hear a clank followed by curses.

The embankment stones are warm as honeycomb.
Acacia clusters in pavement cracks.
A cloud, as in an opening in a forest.
Insane Tour Montparnasse. Midday, which,
To tell the truth, could not have come to pass.

'As I recall, a different emptiness
Was allotted you. You were expected to grow
Up into it.' Steps retreat on the square,
And a bell resounds on this side of the Seine.

'Will we have anything else to talk about?
Here are those same cafés, the soaring feathers,
Which you already knew before you saw them.
Most likely, they've been granted without a purpose.
You live inside the rupture of the map,
Outside the calendar.'
                              Notre Dame's
Grey edge is not as far as I expected;
I see it beneath my feet, in the water, where,
Without rushing, it floats toward my side,
Having renounced the building.
                              'I know
You're trying hard. But what is left for you?
The acoustics here are different.
                              'I was wrong,
This is not Notre Dame.
              'By the way,
Soon, even you will be transformed. The silence
In the receiver, chestnuts, glowing streets
Will perform this task for you. I know,
You will try everything. But then you'll tire.
The barracks in a hundred-mile morass,
The Black Marias, the squeaking boots, barbed wire
Will soon become a newspaper brevier,
A senseless flash in the circuits of consciousness,
Less real than even you, although
You're clearly lacking in reality.'
The Bastille, the colossal sun. It seems
I went against the current.
                              'I will add
Just one more detail: hope does not exist.
There's something more important than hope.'

Berlin Subway. Hallesches Tor

Winter over Europe. The expanse of asphalted fields
Contracts, wrinkles, and splits like a chestnut shell.
The menacing pride of space is spent here. Winter
And the Berlin peninsula. A bone, cardboard, cement.

We see the sky inside out. There are guards on the streets.
A patch stands out on a wall, the blue lamps gleam.
A directionless void. The ball of thread will not lead
Out to alter-existence. Over Europe snow flaps its wings.

You often don't know, after travelling years and miles,
Which shore you will reach. It's all the same, Jericho, Mitte –
The plans of cities change, termites toil,
And a trumpet will never be born of a voiceless whisper.

Turn around, look from yesterday into tomorrow.
There, steeped in the blackened snow, a man grows darker.
He's not destined to see a cardboard wagon crawl
Past Hallesches Tor, having been to nowhere and farther.

East Rock

A beacon, barely visible from afar.
Two enormous boulders by the sea.
A little island, floating in the cove,
Resists the break of day without success.
It recedes, turning into a boat,
Then into a cherry pit. The sky filters
Through the clear cirrus. Flashes of the radar
Brush the axis of the earth at times.

The road has ended, there's nowhere to retreat.
Only space is visible through the gorge,
A cluster of trees tumbles down the banks,
A leaf quivers in the cemetery
Of air. Contours crumble, forms change,
And colour meets up with its destiny,
Attaining the highest red inside the hewed
Cutting between October and September.

Watershed of months! Deadened senses
Of hornbeam groves, eloquence of bluejays!
The roaring blast of a motorcycle starting
At daybreak, five or seven blocks away!
By the cliff, curved like an elk's hide,
Grasses wither, the air becomes hoarfrosted,
So cold and so transparent, that it seems
To need our glance in no way whatsoever.

Today, slightly more clearly than today,
You identify the universe's admixture:
It is born even before our birth,
Grows inside us from the primal cry,
Breaks through the fortress of the arteries,
Pierces the lungs and ripens in the lymph;
We have no sense that tells us this, except
The horror and darkness of the whole body.

A bluejay sings a short song over and over,
Changing the melody ever so slightly,
But there's no repetition and no change
For that which was given once upon a time,
So that, having united error with truth,
Destruction with passion, you would become a piece
Of the permafrost of your epoch, like the bones
In Kolyma, like stones past the Atlantic.

So then, take the shadow along with you,
The black mirror, the barren land of speech,
Choosing freedom every second, since
There is no other form of expiation.
Still the glass of water is not empty,
Still no breeze has creaked the weather vane,
The car at the foot of the slope still does not know
If it will head for the city, or for the north.

Instruction

The flight takes less than an hour. The border guard
gives you no trouble; taking his time, he glances over the passport
(the only card in the never-ending game)
and waves his hand. Of course, a lot can change
in a year, a month or a minute;
there's a risk, albeit not great. Red brick slums
from the Mayerling epoch. A holiday. Portraits in the windows,
not seen for a good decade. Banners, slogans.
The best time in these parts; the authorities have cleared out of the city,
the archives are locked, the orderly is too lazy
to touch the disc with his finger; in all likelihood the prisons
have two or three watchmen left, those particularly in love
with their job. On such a day, a pilot,
not shot down, flies over the land where there's more uranium and steel
than grain; on such a day he lands in the city
to which you certainly won't return. True, he's braver.
November, dark boulevards; without fail, behind the arches, someone
is hiding, just as in a dream. All in all, this reminds one of a dream.

A hill in the mist, but there's no need to climb the hill.
Here, it seems, it is the only one. The flat plains stretch
to the Dnieper, then to the Urals and Gobi. Past the bridge, turn right.
The splendor of the blinded glass, the extinguished lamps,
the art nouveau fences, the old mosques will accompany you. There are
          few passersby.
You remain invisible to them. It's been drizzling for so many days.
A valley, a vast valley, like the bottom of a lagoon.
Stone snails above the doors; octopi and sea lilies
on the cornices; even the river is grey as a mollusc
that has crawled out of its shell.

It hasn't ended, and it won't end. A peasant-faced woman
is selling flowers. A carnation will do.
Here, already, it's not far. Usually the monument has guards,
whose duty it is to confiscate the flowers. But today is a holiday.
They, too, have a right to rest. Exactly thirty years ago,
on the square, there was a gathering (of a thousand? two? There wouldn't have
                  been room, probably, for five),
some with carnations, some probably empty-handed.
What happened afterward has been written in a wealth of books.
To read such books, you had to leave your homeland.
Here and there, perhaps, a split stone can be found,
a pockmarked stretch of granite, the corner of a building lopped off,
but after all these years you need a guide to help you grasp it.

You know little, to tell the truth, about the person on the square:
'having crossed his arms on the armour', 'the walls of Jericho tumble down',
'farther – farther – '. Possibly the best verses on earth.
A Freemason, an artillerist. Lame, with a burned face.
Labiau, Ostrołęka, Wola, Temesvár.
There were a few more battles lost than won.
He died of fever in the town of Aleppo, soon after embracing Islam.

Not one passerby. Put a carnation at his feet,
so that the world may implode like a star, defeated by its own gravity.
The continent collapses into the valley, the valley into the city mist,
the city mist into the square, the square into the monument.
The carnation is the center of it all. Heavy, nothing but neutrons.
When you pass by, two hours later,
it will still be lying on the stone. Or, at least, so it will seem.

A meaningless gesture. You waited thirty years for it.
You changed countries, destinies, friends, but attained your goal.
The people who then assembled on the square (not all of them returned home)
Waited for a century. Even more: a hundred and eight years. What can you do:
These plains, steppes, mist teach you how to wait.

Pestel Street

...*a low dishonest decade*...
W.H. AUDEN

Summer submerges the city,
The glass reflects only dust,
Warm wine trickles
Into the hazy chalice.
The air is flavoured with fading
Cupola gold in the sun.
Algae, like Cyrillic characters,
Blacken the narrow canal.

What do you seek here, poet?
An old balcony, a text
Effaced on the crumbling stucco,
The world, turned into dust.
The untied Gordian knot,
Lime, asphalt and tile,
The gateway mud, the litter
On stairways, the opened door.

Here, where gesture, life,
And sound once coincided,
The flowing crowds now speak
A slightly altered language.
The whiteness of June is throbbing,
And the blind brain, turning
To stone, no longer contains
All the time that was lost.

The new era colours the accent,
The syntax, the architecture,
The droplets of sun on the columns,
The bronzen smile in the bay.
Perhaps only poverty and hunger
Resist the era still,
Perhaps only shadow and fear
Linger on from our youth.

Grow accustomed to swimming in fear,
Just like a fish in the ocean.
Fear is long-lasting here,
Much more enduring than bodies.
Peaceful open squares
Are tasting the haze of noon.
Lime, asphalt, and tile,
Cyrillic on crumbling stucco.

Even now there remains of life
Several copper coins,
Time's change, counted out
By the local absurd bank.
Melody, gesture freeze over.
The prospect disowns the alleys.
It's strange that we saw each other
Somewhat before we expected:

Not in the Vale of Jehoshaphat,
Not in the grove by Lethe,
Not even in the airless universe,
Where, in the manner of gods,
Kelvin and Becquerel rule.
The warmed wine is trickling.
Clouds of sleeplessness float
Over white and hot June.

The crowd and the sound float on,
But the weight of our craft stays the same:
To change time into a stanza,
To concentrate fear into meaning.
Only dust and the voice are throbbing.
The voice has no way of knowing
How much truth can fit
Into its shine and solitude.

In the Fire

in the fire in the fire in the fire in the fire in the fire
where space pulls over to the side and yields to time
cross out my soul make the not me in me expire
that the exalted nothing tasting peace may become
a spark a speck a line and a breach in the fire

in water in water in water in water in water
beneath the cupola filled with echo and ice
today you protect me and hand me out to others
may I not return home don't see me don't break my disguise
where eight bridges sway in the piercing cold in the water

underground underground underground underground underground
where the stone falls apart and the soundless stream stays together
where the winter matures and no colour in green can be found
the body retreats into ash and ash into never
and from never to never the void flows under the ground

in the dark in the dark in the dark in the dark in the dark
our matter becomes dispersed and our air grows slack
all things are ready for death when the syllable sparks
and pressed into fictional paper the letters grow black
in this darkness here in this blindness here in this dark

*   *   *

An enormous book begins to flap like wings in the night:
Black, fire-embossed Exodus, or a dictionary perhaps,
Ciphers, hieroglyphs, numbers... The meaning barred from our sight,
The thing not to be repeated by crystal, swallow, or grass.

Once heavily tilted, the stellar glory floats without direction,
The soul coincides with the century, the century is half-erased.
Time imprisons the soul and space is the body's deception,
And one can no longer draw the line between photo and maze.

Phosphorus, gold, and magnesium! Electric Tuscan sky!
The word loses its fullness, the shadow breaks from the sound.
Latin is dead, there are no singing discs here or on high,
Syntax has crumbled and scattered. Black soil, clay, and sand.

Perhaps only interjections and beats will sort this out.
We've tasted little honey, but lived what's worth living yet:
A garden, a spring, a stone... The brilliance of low-hanging clouds,
Nothing more sudden than existence and nothing more true than death.

Never ask why. Only he who pulled the door slightly ajar
To the place without hill or star, or certainty of grace,
Drives time away with a shield, like a fallen Etruscan at war,
Scoops up meaning in his hand, and washes his cancelled face.

* * *

Half a mile away, where the highways cross,
A flame is struck up by a range of flint.
The ice, quivering above the springs, thaws,
And the reflection of the ash grove doesn't fit.

It's still too early for the bitterest stroke,
The banks will harden in transparent mist,
And even God, once simulating smoke,
Will dissipate. But that is not my point.

Believe in winter. Drink the blessed cold.
Take pride in knowing that your home is lost.
Just like the ones who huddle in a boat,
Breathe darkness and the clarity of salt.

Sleep envelops Ithaca's hills and dales,
And injured children sleep without a murmur,
And only death will finally prevail,
And wet snow, and music, and nothing ever.

Tu, Felix Austria

In this city, weary
of saving humankind, where many cures
have been imposed upon the many nerves
of those who tell their sticky
dreams through shortened breath,
timed to the hour, softened
by sofas in the office,
where aging Europe's unbeloved
son conceived of death,

he who was so rashly
rejected by the artists' guild – today
the whirlpool swings the still boat into sway,
and the banks of the river swing
under the twin rows
of chestnut trees. In a café,
you hear the viral sputter of last year's rock,
and not ruins, but the ponderous baroque,
along with a star

stuck on the lofty balcony
bears witness to the arrogance of this land.
The rhythm rocks the consciousness to sleep.
The concave air of the square
slides into your eye –
so transparent, it seems
your feet swing like a pendulum,
and only music and pulse, in amalgam,
give you a hand.

You are blinded
by the colour of the clouds; ambling
under arches; almost blended
with granite, dust, lilac blossoms,
you find no common words
with this euphonic chime;
too suddenly an outcast of your time,
not sure whether this is a curse
or a blessing.

Not straightening his back,
Sisyphus can rest
on the mountain's peak,
detaching his palm in terror
from the flaring stone –
the burden which for eons
wrecked him, then tamed him,
now stuck in gravel, aimless
and nameless.

It is sunny and still.
In the open, a dog rose spills
into blossom, and at last
there is no need to joust
with destiny,
rake the grass, stumble, slide
down the steep siliceous shoulder,
and youth slips, a moment later,
from your memory.

And if only one broken
sentence still disturbs the soul,
maybe these are just the strokes
of the taut bell 'Bella
gerant...' And if at night
a wretched raft, about to be rolled
over by Austrus's rage,
is launched out into the sea,
others, not we,

will perish there. Blood fades;
a tank turns into dust.
An era has ended; the plague must
choose new lands. The train
no longer enters the terminal
where fire and space are fraternal,
where machine guns, speaking in Morse,
answer Moses and Christ
in snapping retorts.

The baroque celestial cloth
sinks over the Habsburg fortress.
Only beyond the horizon
where the air wounds, where a man
crawls into a hole, where stone
breaks into sand, where lead
so swiftly meets flesh, – between
Franz Ferdinand and today
there is no gulf.

The foliage, shattered
into splinters, like blackened plaster,
binds the mouth, and Saturn
is saturated with his sperm,
just as when time was first spawned.
And yet not here does torment
fuse late evening and dawn,
exceeding the terms
set forth for mortals.

In a camp, on a stone field,
refugees taste the darker
air of freedom, dreaming
visionless, having a few
happy hours to spend,
while those whom a bullet spent
(and saved) probably see starker
dreams, and yet seem stronger,
and more content.

Death is not here, she always looms.
The tones of the bells come closer;
she lives in granite, heat, wine,
and bread, in chestnuts entwined
with acacias. She roams
in dreams. History is part
of death. Galileo, not Hegel, was right:
eppur si muove. A dense, charred
sphere revolves into night.

What at first seemed real is just a denial
of time. There is no revival
in sleep. Nothing and clouds extend
through the window. Death
is not here. Death is at hand.
She rides around in the cage of the room,
crosses out the next calendar date,
then looks in the mirror and meets
you face to fate.

But while she still dallies in blackish glass air,
Sisyphus is needed here,
Here, in this insomniac city,
uninclined to distinguish the petty
from the things that matter, to unearth
the root of the foretold myth,
and await, without hope,
the trumpets of the Lord
on the diamond-sharp slope.

*   *   *

(to Maurice Friedberg)

A projector flickers in the somewhat cramped hall.
Only three viewers. Four, including one
who came from far away, who suggested this film
to his students. The oblong box preserves
a country where not even stones (or friends,
for that matter) remember him. Several languages
jostle in the subconscious. Garlands, faces,

and banners overcome the hanging blackness.
It's all unruly and festive. He who grew up
in a feastless state cannot bring himself
to look at the screen. He already knows
what's in store: dark warm bloodstains
and mud. No telling them apart, no telling
letters from fire, or truth from nothingness.

The heat drags down the university town.
Jasmines, fainting into a nod, surround
the gravel-covered paths and sweaty lawns,
where the water sprinkler fires away in series.
Distances grow. The newcomer tells his neighbour,
'But everything turned out well in the end –'
and tries hard to believe what he is saying.

Henkus Hapenčkus, In Memoriam

(for Pranas Morkus)

A greeting isn't worth it. Only a true nobody can manage
to shoulder the weight of non-existence. Nothing is more unchanging
than his loneliness. Motors strain to catch the air, wailing
between the circuit court and the stairway to the hillside,
across the graveyard, where buttercups, poisonous and wan, wither
and stone and metal avoid those dates that could never happen.
Well then, we met again, under the narrow prospect's lindens.
What you are and will be is only the bent corner
of a cheap plate, letters in a sun-baked store window,
a bunch of vowels and consonants, ripped from the void's phonebook
not even the transparent shadow, mirrored in the waters of Lethe,

not even a contour glimmering deep below the liquid surface,
in the well where a single glow holds the stars of Ursus Major.
The city has not even forgotten the one 'who never existed'.
Unnoticed, you will extend this day, as you did the others.
Weirder to the passing glance than even Odysseus, Noah,
Peter Pan, Hamlet or Winnie-the-Pooh, barely
finding a place in space, where the ageing consciousness, dodging,
brightening like a gap in the air, follows the dodging asphalt,
you coincide with anything. You've been imbibed by the faded,
arid pre-war stucco, the sterile fog of summer,
that didn't manage to thicken, but vanished that very minute.

On this side of the bitter river, past hope and desperation,
blind to your incantations (as you to my native language)
I, a third-class god, try to blow soul into letters,
soul sketched roughly by the chisel of a provincial master,
to imagine a country where the throne has been claimed by absence,

the faceless terrain entrusted to you. Its panoramas
do not lend themselves to pen, tempera or sanguine –
there all fates are alike, each revenge equal to its cousin,
a slope turns into a trace, a house – into something smaller,
but perhaps with the same dimensions. A gram is a gram there also,
a metre equals a metre, vodka will still get you tipsy.

If peoples are preserved over there – one-fifth Pole or Prussian,
eternally frozen into the dulled ice of the nameplate,
Henkus exists in the beyond, not visited by Dante,
belonging to no one in spirit, to Hades only in phonetics,
a chauffeur, a journalist, a petty informer, forgotten.
How many crumpled dresses, linen awash with sperm,
how many colourless glasses by the non-tavern's non-window,
kicks, punches in the face, swear words, youth without purpose,
semi-starved Augusts and bone-breaking Decembers
fit into the dense nameplate. And words are all of existence,
and the evening martins patch the worn-through sky of Kaunas.

A light with the spectrum erased, a motif depleted of timbres,
he roams in the dips of our talk, so as not to become the topic.
Only for us the trumpet keeps on playing, and the yellow
flame still shines through the tangled system of linden branches.
In their spaces we watch an empty block, doubly empty
because Henkus stamps there; he relieves himself, unembarrassed,
on the no longer visible corner, squeezes onto the bus,
unborn and undisappearing, tasting unconditional freedom
to which – like it or not – we all have to grow accustomed,
albeit still subject to time, albeit still trying to linger
on a fate that never existed. He was one of our brethren.

San Michele

Two-faced, just like Janus, the crack
leans up against the boat, hurled by the churning
waves up onto the wharf. Thus forms the link
between eye, cupola and firmament,
The motor thrashes in the midst of desert,
and the corroded starboard crushes the clay,
where Orcus greets us with coagulated walls
and the June sun, transparent as the sky.
Grass and stone. Same island as before.
And, turning to stone, a wanderer lends his ear
to the heaping of the silence on the bush,
the thick sound of sphere answering sphere,
the limestone pushing its way into the waves,
while the consciousness is wakened into feeling
no longer by a jab of pain, but still
something other than water, tree, or steamship.

The Member of the Landing Crew

The hardest thing to do was to hide the boats they had dragged up onto the sand,
to cut up the tight rubber, shove the scraps under the bushes,
to ignore the prickly rain that comes before the dawn,

inundating the spine. The low pines kept silent across the dunes.
When the line moved, he sighed. His oesophagus
recalled the memory of yesterday's seasickness,

and his shoulders, the strap of the backpack. Penicillin, binoculars,
ammunition, written off of army storage the year before last,
a letter from an old minister with the words 'long live unity',

a radio. Never having been to this seaside before, he sank
in the sand, pressed the pine needles, aligned himself with his friend's jacket,
knowing his homeland by the shape of the cumulus cloud.

*

The needle of the compass danced out the ritual *klumpakojis* dance.
Eight kilometres down the road, next to the deserted farm,
he'd have to encounter the Bear, the Fern Blossom and the Goat –

nicknames from fables. An unfamiliar group stomped its feet
in the glade. The commander, whom he had seen somewhere before
in the unfinished war, said the password. Alleviated,

his companions disappeared in the dugout, but he lagged behind. His boot
slipped on the mossy tussock by the stream, and the blow,
missing the back of his head, landed on his elbow. Grabbing

his holster in a rush, he was able to feel
the muscles in his kneeling leg tense; he saw the black aperture
before his eyes and grasped: well, that guy is quicker.

154

*

His brains, clinging to the stem of a reed, dried up long ago.
The rest soaked into the sand. At least he's lucky
the secret service couldn't extract any codes from it,

since, were it not for the wet hummock, probably he, like his two friends,
who were less fortunate that morning, say what you will,
would have misled his people in the dark games of the Great

Powers, would have reached old age in the stinging cigarette smoke
of a provincial café with a hundred grams of cognac,
trying to persuade everyone, including himself, that he saved

young people from bullets and nooses – or, maybe
having been across the Arctic Circle and back, he would have striven
in vain, in ignorant offices for compensation for lost time.

It's better the way it turned out. No cross, no memory.
The trucks stagger on the bumpy strip of gravel road
a few steps away from the place where it all happened.

The sweat-soaked drivers play the brakes like piano keys,
an axe is heard in the pine forest, the farmstead walls turn white,
the cuckoo promises we'll live long yet;

three times or maybe four times as long as he.
Whoever died will never return; what's lost is gone.
Only the scraps of the rubber boat under the seaside willow

still await the Lord's judgment, and the outline of the cloud,
exactly the same as then, crawls over the forest glade,
and the algae sway in the stream, which he didn't reach then.

A View from an Alley

Where gooseberries used to grow, new landlords have turned up the soil.
The courtyard is tightly sealed from the street's chestnut trees
by a dark bluish double fence. All dimensions have shrunk,
except for time. There was more space here than childhood alone can explain.
Squinting, you can still climb the dissolved staircase
up to the attic, where the floor still squeaks under your cousin's steps.
For long? He asked us then. *Only for one night* (but that happened later).
On the first floor a mass of mirror turned to stone, easily meshing
the hoarfrost of a faraway storm, the crown of a plum tree, a flask
rich with dense scents. These early insomnias: the chime
through the wall, helping us understand that everything passes,
but not soon; that time depends on speech,
that the worst case scenario turns out a little less
than what we can bear. A heaven of photographs behind the door.
In one I make out a shadow with a glass of cherry juice
and a dog. These snapshots still live somewhere,
although few people today would be able to figure them out.
The dog is buried in the corner of the kitchen garden
(now I cannot see the place behind the double fence)
and the shadow, pressing the glass to his mouth, still glides
on the surface of objects, next to the ribbed wallpaper,
the destitute greenery, the littered years, which belong
not to him, nor to the new landlords, a little more real than he.
No one knows what matches this dead space,
this empty cell in the net of alleys:
indifference or pain? Strangely, they coincide.

Notes

A New Postcard from the City of K. (22): The Pregel is a river in Königsberg. The Natangians were an old Prussian tribe, closely related to Lithuanians, who lived to the south of Königsberg. Mantas (Heinrich Monte) was the leader of the insurrection of Natangians and other tribes against the German rule. He tried to raze Königsberg in the 13th century. Aismares is the old Prussian (as well as Lithuanian) name for Vistula Bay. The poem is a response to 'Postcard from the City of K.' by Joseph Brodsky.

Dunes at Watermill (25): The three stories retold in this poem are taken from the lives of the author's colleagues. Watermill is a township on Long Island.

Arrival in Atlantis (29): The poem's setting is Baltiysk, formerly an East Prussian (now Russian) naval harbour. An imagined meeting with the late poet Joseph Brodsky (who visited Baltiysk in 1963) is depicted.

For an Older Poet (30): This poem refers to the poet's late father Antanas Venclova, a Soviet poet. More broadly, it is a meditation on a generation of Lithuanian poets.

Two Apocrypha (32): The second section of this poem makes reference to a Polish soldier who was taken as a POW by the Soviets in 1939.

The Junction (35): A geographic junction where the borders of Lithuania, the Russian district of Kaliningrad (formerly East Prussia) and Poland meet.

After the Lecture (37): The woman depicted in this poem is Anna Akhmatova. *Deus conservat omnia* ('God preserves everything') is a Latin motto that was inscribed on the gate of the house where she lived; it was also used as an epigraph for her 'Poem Without a Hero'.

Užupis (41): Užupis is a district in Vilnius, a meeting place for avant-garde artists and poets.

Theseus Leaving Athens (42): In Greek mythology, Theseus is often associated with a carved ivory-hilted sword. For the purposes of this poem, the Minotaur is pierced by bronze, the material of weapons during this age. Theseus was exiled from Athens and then killed by Lycomedes.

On a Mountain Ridge Near Jordan (44): A monologue in the voice of Moses before his death. It takes place on Mount Nebo (now in Jordan), where Moses died before he could enter the Promised Land. All biblical references appear in the Old Testament.

Discipline and Punish. A Visit to the Detention Centre IZ-45/1 (48): The title refers to Michel Foucault's work, *Discipline and Punish*. Its setting is the Kresty ('Crosses') prison in Petersburg, which one can now visit for a fee. The avenue 'disfigured by modernity' is Litejnyj Avenue, along which Akhmatova had to walk on her way from Fontanny Dom to Kresty. Nabokov's father was imprisoned in Kresty and after emigrating, was murdered in Berlin. The poem also refers to Nikolay Zabolotsky, the author of 'Somewhere in a field near Magadan...' and to Joseph Brodsky.

From Landwehrkanal to Spree (50): The setting is Berlin after the fall of the Wall. Huguenots played a role in the city's life in the 17th and 18th centuries. The émigré quoted in the poem is Vladislav Khodasevich, a Russian poet who lived in Berlin in the 1920s.

Ormond Quay (53): About Ireland's past and recent renewal. James Joyce and the Martello Tower, which appears at the beginning of *Ulysses*, are referred to in the poem.

Homage to Shqiperia (56): This poem is dedicated to Shqiperia, Albania. Its city Durrës (Epidamnos in antiquity) has a surviving Roman amphitheatre, and was the location for Plautus' comedy *Menaechmi*. The sponger Peniculus, one of its characters, appears at the beginning of the poem and at its end, where he paraphrases Heraclitus and Socrates. Bunkers constructed in the days of the dictator Enver Hoxha are a distinctive feature of the Albanian landscape.

Anno Domini 2002 (58): On the collapse of the World Trade Center buildings. W.H. Auden's poem 'September 1, 1939', is quoted. The Statue of Liberty appears in the first stanza. The time is New Year's Eve.

La Baigneuse (60): Francesco Guardi was an 18th-century Italian painter famed for his oil sketches of Venice and its lagoons.

Commentary (62): 'where the stairwell's shaft is guarded by steel nets': in the former Soviet Union, most, if not all, stairwells in prisons and KGB buildings were enclosed in steel nets, to prevent prisoner suicide attempts.

In the Lake Region (66): The location is outside of Berlin between Wannsee and Potsdam. The poem's subject is the Wannsee Conference House, where the policy for Hitler's 'Final Solution' was consolidated.

Limbo (67): The setting is the main square in Kraków, Poland. Pelion and Ossa are from Homer's *Odyssey*.

He Who Turned Around at the Border (69): A poem about Orpheus and Eurydice. Thrace is the land where the Maenads tore Orpheus to pieces.

Antonio Vivaldi (71): *Se parto, se resto* is an aria by Antonio Vivaldi.

Las Meninas (72): 'Las Meninas' is a painting by Velásquez. The analysis referred to by Michel Foucault appears in his book *Words and Objects*.

Verses for a Child's Birth (75): Birnam Wood appears in Shakespeare's *Macbeth*. The Ceryneian Hind was the fourth labour of Hercules. The quoted poem by George Herbert is 'Church Monuments'.

Pastoral (77): A poem set in the swamps near Berlin.

WINTER DIALOGUE (*pages* 79-156)

Winter Dialogue (82): On the Polish uprising of 1970. According to an old Lithuanian belief, one can establish the year of the uprising from tree rings, since the ring of the preceding year is very narrow.

Nel Mezzo Del Cammin Di Nostra Vita (90): Konstantin Bogatyrev (1925-76), a poet and dissident, was murdered at the door of his Moscow apartment, presumably by KGB agents.

Shoots of grass pierce one's face and hands (100): This poem is about Osip Mandelstam's period of exile in Voronezh, as he awaited his final imprisonment and death.

A Poem About Friends (114): On the 1968 demonstration in Red Square against the Soviet invasion of Czechoslovakia. 'A hole in stone stairs' was made in the Lubyanka prison in Moscow by the feet of many thousands of prisoners.

Autumn in Copenhagen (119): 'A leaking uranium whale' refers to a Soviet nuclear submarine that ran aground in 1981 on the Swedish coastline.

Sheremetyevo, 1977 (123): 'A poet from these parts' is Fyodor Tyutchev.

Instruction (136): On a visit to Budapest during the 30th anniversary of the 1956 Hungarian Uprising (the date of the visit coincided with the anniversary of the October Revolution). The quoted poem, by Cyprian Norwid, is dedicated to the 19th-century revolutionary Józef Bem. The events of 1956 started at Bem's monument.

Pestel Street (139): Joseph Brodsky lived on Pestel Street in Leningrad before going into exile. The poem refers to the author's stay in Leningrad in 1988, during Gorbachev's *perestroika* period.

Tu, Felix Austria (145): *'Bella gerant alii, tu, felix Austria, nubes'* (Let others make war, you, happy Austria, make love), an old motto of the Austrian Empire.

In Memoriam, Henkus Hapenčkus (151): In the window of a Kaunas funeral parlour for several decades there was an advertisement – a plate with the name 'Henkus Hapenčkus'. Such a name does not exist in Lithuanian. As the individual's dates were also absurd, it appears the shopkeepers had done their best to avoid any coincidence with a living person. The poem's subject therefore never existed.

The Member of the Landing Crew (154): After the Second World War, some Lithuanian émigrés, helped by English and Swedish intelligence services, attempted to land on Lithuania's shores and join the anti-Soviet partisan movement. More often than not, they were met by Soviet units posing as partisans, and either killed or drafted into the KGB. This poem describes one such individual, Justinas Dočkus.

Bibliography

Tomas Venclova: *The Junction: Selected Poems*

The dates of first appearance in periodicals and subsequent book publication are noted in parentheses.

The Junction

Winter Dialogue

A Poem About Memory: IN *Kalbos* (1966/1972).

Winter Dialogue: IN *Kalbos* (1971/1972).

I was welcomed by twilight and cold: IN *Kalbos* (1971/1972).

To The Memory Of a Poet. Variation: IN *Kalbos* (1969/1972).

Nel Mezzo Del Cammin Di Nostra Vita: IN *98* (1977/1977).

The Shield Of Achilles: IN *98* (1972/1977).

The Eleventh Canto: IN *98* (1977/1977).

We've been seized by the pull of the universe: IN 98 (1977/1977).

Glimmer a smile, stand still, then take the path back home: IN *98* (1970/1977).

All night, sleep was equivalent to time: IN *98* (1966/1977).

Shoots of grass pierce one's face and hands: IN *Kalbos* (1972/1972).

To the squares on our walls and floors: IN *Kalbos* (1966/1972).

Desist, desist. The crumbling sentence dies: IN *98* (1977/1977).

An Attempt at Describing a Room: IN *Kalbos* (1972/1972).

Sestina: IN *98* (1977/1977).

Ode to a City: IN *98* (1975/1977).

Two Poems About Love: IN *98* (1974/1977).

Although the well is bottomless and steep: IN *98* (1973/1977).

In the indigent cities, it's time to leave friends behind us: IN *Kalbos* (1968/1972).

Ghetto: IN *98* (1977/1977).

A Poem About Friends: IN *98* (1969/1977).

Thanksgiving Day: IN *Tank.* (1980/1990).

Autumn in Copenhagen: IN *Tank.* (1983/1990).

Sheremetyevo, 1977: IN *Tank.* (1985/1990).

Bit by bit, at the edge of the unforeseen land: IN *Tank.* (1980/1990).

I have learned to see in the dark: IN *Tank.* (1988/1990).

A Museum in Hobart: IN *Tank.* (1978/1990).

Before the middle of July, Paris: IN *Tank.* (1979/1990).

Berlin Subway. Hallesches Tor: IN *Tank.* (1979/1990).

East Rock: IN *Tank.* (1985/1990).

Instruction: IN *Tank.* (1987/1990).

Pestel Street: IN *Tank.* (1988/1990).

In the Fire: IN *Tank.* (1980/1990).

An enormous book begins to flap: IN *Tank.* (1987/1990).

Half a mile away, where the highways cross: IN *Tank.* (1987/1990).

Tu, Felix Austria: IN *Rink.* (1992/1999).

A projector flickers in the somewhat cramped hall: IN *Rink.* (1991/1999).

Henkus Hapenčkus, In Memoriam: IN *Reg.* (1997/1998).

San Michele: IN *Reg.* (1997/1998).

The Member of the Landing Crew: IN *Reg.* (1996/1998).

A View From an Alley: IN *Reg.* (1995/1998).

Tomas Venclova: Selected Bibliography

WORKS IN ENGLISH

Lithuanian Literature: A Survey, trans. Algirdas Landsbergis (New York: Lithuanian National Foundation, Inc., 1979).

Aleksander Wat: Life and Art of an Iconoclast (New Haven and London: Yale University Press, 1996). Written in English.

Winter Dialogue, trans. Diana Senechal, (Evanston, Ill.: Northwestern University Press, 1997).

Forms of Hope (Essays), various translators (Riverdale-on-Hudson: Sheep Meadow Press, 1999).

Vilnius: City Guide, trans. Aušra Simanavičiūtė (Vilnius: R. Paknio leidykla, 2001).

Tomas Venclova (Poems), trans. Laima Sruoginis (Klaipėda: House of Artists, 2002).

The Junction: Selected Poems, ed. Ellen Hinsey, trans. Ellen Hinsey, Constantine Rusanov and Diana Senechal (Tarset: Bloodaxe Books, 2008).

SELECTED WORKS IN LITHUANIAN

Raketos, planetos ir mes (*Rockets, Planets and Us*), (Vilnius: Valstybinė grožinė s literatūros leidykla, 1962).

Golemas, arba dirbtinis žmogus (*The Golem or Artificial Man, Discussions on Cybernetics*), (Vilnius: Vaga, 1965).

Kalbos ženklas (*Sign of Speech*, Poems), (Vilnius: Vaga, 1972).

98 eilėraščiai (*98 Poems*), (Chicago: Algimanto Mackaus knygų leidimo fondas, 1977).

Balsai: Iš pasaulinės poezijos. Sudarė ir išvertė Tomas Venclova (Selected Translations), (Southfield, Michigan: Ateitis, 1979).

Lietuva pasaulyje (*Lithuania in the World*, Essays), (Chicago: Akademinės skautijos leidykla, 1981).

Tekstai apie tekstus (*Texts on Texts*, Essays), (Chicago: Algimanto Mackaus knygų leidimo fondas, 1985).

Tankėjanti šviesa (*The Condensing Light*, Poems), (Chicago: Algimanto Mackaus knygų leidimo fondas, 1990).

Pašnekesys žiemą (*Winter Dialogue*, Poems/Translations) (Vilnius: Vaga, 1991).

Vilties formos (*Forms of Hope*, Essays and Writings), (Vilnius: Lietuvos rašytojų sąjungos leidykla, 1991).

Reginys iš alėjos (*A View from an Alley*, Poems), (Vilnius: Baltos lankos, 1998).

Rinktinė (*Selected Poems*), (Vilnius: Baltos lankos, 1999).

Manau, kad...: Pokalbiai su Tomu Venclova (I think that... Conversations with Tomas Venclova), (Vilnius: Baltos lankos, 2000).

Guenter Grass, Czesław Miłosz, Wisława Szymborska, Tomas Venclova (*On the Future of Memory*, Essays), (Vilnius: Baltos lankos, 2001).

Vilnius: Vadovas po miestą (*Vilnius City Guide*), (Vilnius: R. Paknio leidykla, 2001).

Ligi Lietuvos 10 000 kilometrų: Iš kelionės dienoraščių (*10,000 Kilometres to Lithuania*, Travel Writing), (Vilnius: Baltos lankos, 2003).

Sankirta (*The Junction*, Poems), (Vilnius: Lietuvos rašytojų sąjungos leidykla, 2005).

Kitaip (*Otherwise*, Selected Translations), (Vilnius, Lietuvos rašytojų sąjungos leidykla, 2006).

Vilniaus vardai (*People from Vilnius*, Biographies), (Vilnius, R. Paknio leidykla, 2006).

THE TRANSLATORS

Ellen Hinsey was born in Boston in 1960. She has lived in Paris since 1987, and teaches on the faculty of the French graduate school, the École Polytechnique, and Skidmore College's Paris programme. She is the author of *Update on the Descent* (Finalist, 2007 National Poetry Series, USA / Bloodaxe Books, UK, 2009), *The White Fire of Time* (Wesleyan University Press, USA, 2002 / Bloodaxe Books, UK, 2003) and *Cities of Memory*, which was awarded the Yale Series of Younger Poets Prize in 1995. Her poems and essays have appeared in many publications including *The New York Times*, *The New Yorker*, *Poetry Review*, *Poetry* and *The Paris Review*, as well as in French, German, Italian, Serbian and Danish journals. Her translations of French poetry were awarded Poetry's Union League Civic and Arts Poetry Prize and she has published collaborative translations from Romanian and Finnish. Her translations of contemporary French fiction and memoir are published with Riverhead/Penguin Books. She has received a Rona Jaffe Foundation Award, a Lannan Foundation Award and a Berlin Prize Fellowship from the American Academy in Berlin.

Constantine Rusanov was born in Nikolayev, in the Ukraine, in 1979. He holds a B.A. from Amherst College in English literature and is currently writing a dissertation on Joseph Brodsky's interlingual poetics at Yale University. In addition to Tomas Venclova, he has also translated selections of Osip Mandelstam, Marina Tsvetaeva, Boris Pasternak, Maximilian Voloshin and Vladimir Mayakovsky (into English) and W.H. Auden, Emily Dickinson and Tomas Venclova (into Russian). He is a recipient of the Nina Berberova Award (Yale University) and the PEN American Center Translation Grant (2006).

Diana Senechal was born in Tucson and holds a Ph.D in Slavic Languages and Literatures from Yale University. Her translations have appeared in publications such as *The New York Review of Books*, *The Partisan Review*, *Orient Express*, *2B: A Journal of Ideas* and *Metamorphosis*. Her selected translations of Tomas Venclova, *Winter Dialogue*, first appeared with Northwestern University Press in 1997. She has also translated selections by Anna Akhmatova, Bella Akhmadulina, Marina Tsvetaeva and Aleksandr Kushner. She has been an invited participant at the International Miłosz Festival and PEN International. Her poetry and fiction have appeared in numerous publications. She lives in Brooklyn and teaches English to immigrant students. Her teaching and performance work have been featured in *The New York Times*.